Editor

Mary S. Jones, M.A.

Managing Editor

Karen J. Goldfluss, M.S. Ed.

Cover Artist

Brenda DiAntonis

Art Production Manager

Kevin Barnes

Art Coordinator

Renée Christine Yates

Imaging

James Edward Grace
Ricardo Martinez

Publisher

Mary D. Smith, M.S. Ed.

Correlations to the Common Core Standards can be found at *http://www.teachercreated.com/ standards/*.

- Over 150 nonfiction and fiction passages
- Follow-up questions for each passage target essential comprehension skills.
- Ideal for test preparation!

Author

Sarah Kartchner Clark, M.A.

Teacher Created Resources, Inc.
6421 Industry Way
Westminster, CA 92683
www.teachercreated.com

ISBN: 978-1-4206-3491-4

©2006 Teacher Created Resources, Inc.
Reprinted, 2013

Made in U.S.A.

Table of Contents

Table of Contents

Introduction

The goal of this book is to improve students' reading and comprehension skills. The more experience a child has with reading and comprehending, the better reader and problem solver he or she will be. *Daily Warm-Ups: Reading* contains a variety of passages to be read on a daily basis. Each passage is followed by comprehension questions. The questions that follow the passages are based on Bloom's Taxonomy and allow for higher-level thinking skills. Making this book a part of your daily classroom agenda can help your students' reading and comprehension abilities improve dramatically.

Nonfiction and Fiction

Daily Warm-Ups: Reading is divided into two sections: nonfiction and fiction. It is important for students to be exposed to a variety of reading genres and formats. The nonfiction section is divided into five categories. These categories are animals, biography, American history, science, and current events. By reading these nonfiction passages, your students will be exposed to a variety of nonfiction information, as well as questions to stimulate thinking on these subjects.

The fiction section of the book is also divided into five categories. These categories are fairy tales/folklore, historical fiction, contemporary realistic fiction, mystery/suspense/adventure, and fantasy. Each story is followed by questions to stimulate thinking on the plot, characters, vocabulary, and sequence.

Comprehension Questions

Comprehension is the primary goal of any reading task. Students who comprehend what they read perform better both on tests and in life. The follow-up questions after each passage are written to encourage students to improve in recognizing text structure, visualizing, summarizing, and learning new vocabulary. Each of these skills can be found in scope-and-sequence charts as well as standards for reading comprehension. The different types of questions in *Daily Warm-Ups: Reading* are geared to help students with the following skills:

- Recognize the main idea
- Identify details
- Recall details
- Summarize
- Describe characters and character traits
- Classify and sort into categories
- Compare and contrast
- Make generalizations
- Draw conclusions
- Recognize fact
- Apply information to new situations
- Recognize sequence
- Understand vocabulary

Introduction

Readability

Each of the reading passages in *Daily Warm-Ups: Reading* varies in difficulty to meet the various reading levels of your students. The passages have been categorized as follows: below grade level, at grade level, and above grade level. (See Leveling Chart on page 175.)

Record Keeping

Use the tracking sheet on page 6 to record which warm-up exercises you have given to your students. Or, distribute copies of the sheet for students to keep their own records. Use the certificate on page 176 as you see fit. You can use the certificate as a reward for students completing a certain number of warm-up exercises. Or, you may choose to distribute the certificates to students who complete the warm-up exercises with 100% accuracy.

How to Make the Most of This Book

Here are some simple tips, which you may have already thought of, already implemented, or may be new to you. They are only suggestions to help you make your students as successful in reading as possible.

- Read through the book ahead of time so you are familiar with each portion. The better you understand how the book works, the easier it will be to answer students' questions.

- Set aside a regular time each day to incorporate *Daily Warm-Ups* into your routine. Once the routine is established, students will look forward to and expect to work on reading strategies at that particular time.

- Make sure that any amount of time spent on *Daily Warm-Ups* is positive and constructive. This should be a time of practicing for success and recognizing it as it is achieved.

- Allot only about 10 minutes to *Daily Warm-Ups*. Too much time will not be useful; too little time will create additional stress.

- Be sure to model the reading and question-answering process at the beginning of the year. Model pre-reading questions, reading the passage, highlighting information that refers to the questions, and eliminating answers that are obviously wrong. Finally, refer back to the text once again, to make sure the answers chosen are the best ones.

- Create and store overheads of each lesson so that you can review student work, concepts, and strategies as quickly as possible.

- Utilize peer tutors who have strong skills for peer interaction to assist with struggling students.

- Offer small group time to students who need extra enrichment or opportunities for questions regarding the text. Small groups will allow many of these students, once they are comfortable with the format, to achieve success independently.

- Adjust the procedures, as you see fit, to meet the needs of all your students.

Tracking Sheet

NONFICTION

Animals		Biography		American History		Science		Currents Events	
Page 9		Page 25		Page 41		Page 57		Page 72	
Page 10		Page 26		Page 42		Page 58		Page 73	
Page 11		Page 27		Page 43		Page 59		Page 74	
Page 12		Page 28		Page 44		Page 60		Page 75	
Page 13		Page 29		Page 45		Page 61		Page 76	
Page 14		Page 30		Page 46		Page 62		Page 77	
Page 15		Page 31		Page 47		Page 63		Page 78	
Page 16		Page 32		Page 48		Page 64		Page 79	
Page 17		Page 33		Page 49		Page 65		Page 80	
Page 18		Page 34		Page 50		Page 66		Page 81	
Page 19		Page 35		Page 51		Page 67		Page 82	
Page 20		Page 36		Page 52		Page 68		Page 83	
Page 21		Page 37		Page 53		Page 69		Page 84	
Page 22		Page 38		Page 54		Page 70		Page 85	
Page 23		Page 39		Page 55		Page 71		Page 86	
Page 24		Page 40		Page 56					

FICTION

Fairy Tales/ Folklore		Historical Fiction		Contemporary Realistic Fiction		Mystery/Suspense/ Adventure		Fantasy	
Page 89		Page 105		Page 120		Page 136		Page 152	
Page 90		Page 106		Page 121		Page 137		Page 153	
Page 91		Page 107		Page 122		Page 138		Page 154	
Page 92		Page 108		Page 123		Page 139		Page 155	
Page 93		Page 109		Page 124		Page 140		Page 156	
Page 94		Page 110		Page 125		Page 141		Page 157	
Page 95		Page 111		Page 126		Page 142		Page 158	
Page 96		Page 112		Page 127		Page 143		Page 159	
Page 97		Page 118		Page 128		Page 144		Page 160	
Page 98		Page 114		Page 129		Page 145		Page 161	
Page 99		Page 115		Page 130		Page 146		Page 162	
Page 100		Page 116		Page 131		Page 147		Page 163	
Page 101		Page 117		Page 132		Page 148		Page 164	
Page 102		Page 118		Page 133		Page 149		Page 165	
Page 103		Page 119		Page 134		Page 150		Page 166	
Page 104				Page 135		Page 151			

NONFICTION

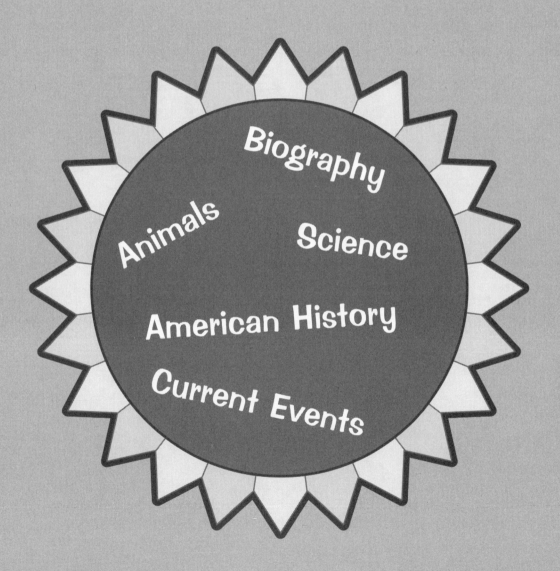

Biography

Animals

Science

American History

Current Events

JUNE BUGS

Have you ever seen a metallic green bug buzzing around in the summertime? You were probably looking at a June bug. June bugs get their name because they emerge as adults at the beginning of summer. It takes a year for a June bug to complete its full life cycle.

A June bug is an insect with six legs and is usually about 15 to 22 cm long. It has a dull, metallic-green body with wings. Its underside is light brown or black. The June bug is part of the beetle (coleopteran) family. This beetle can be found all over the United States, but it is prominent in the northeastern states. The beetle loves to feed on ripening fruit. They will gather in clusters and eat ripened apples, peaches, pears, or any other fruit. When the beetle is still a grub, it will feed on decaying matter, grass, and other plants. These grubs will also go underground to eat plants such as sweet potatoes and carrots.

In the past, a fun summer activity for many children was to catch June bugs. Children would tie a string to one of the legs and then let the June bug fly around while holding the string. This provided hours of entertainment for children. Some children still participate in this activity today.

STORY QUESTIONS

1. According to this reading passage, why would someone want to catch a June bug?
   a. They are trying to keep the June bug from eating their plants.
   b. The June bug can bring good luck.
   c. The June bug can provide entertainment.
   d. The June bug likes to live in captivity.

2. This passage is mostly about . . .
   a. protecting your lawn and fruit trees from June bugs.
   b. good extermination practices.
   c. the anatomy of a June bug.
   d. general information about June bugs.

3. According to the passage, what do adult June bugs eat?
   a. They eat seeds and seedlings.
   b. They eat ripening fruit.
   c. They feed on the grass.
   d. They dig underground to eat sweet potatoes and carrots.

4. How did the June bug get its name?
   a. It is named after the famous first lady June Cleveland.
   b. It is a cousin to the ladybug.
   c. It lays its eggs in June.
   d. It is an adult beetle in the summer months.

THE ARMADILLO

The armadillo is probably one of the most unusual-looking animals. It looks a lot like the dinosaurs that used to walk the Earth. Armadillos can live in many places throughout the United States and other parts of the world, but they are most prominent in the state of Texas.

The armadillo has a very tough shell with bands of very strong tissue. These bands are able to slide over each other, which allows the armadillo to roll up like a ball. This is how the armadillo is able to protect itself. It is like the armadillo is protected by a shield of armor. Most animals are unable to break through this tough skin. An armadillo lives in a burrow that it digs itself. The armadillo has to live in places where the dirt is easy to dig; otherwise, it cannot dig itself a home. They have very strong claws that help them dig.

The armadillo's main diet is insects. They eat ants, termites, beetles, grubs, worms, and other small insects. These animals are also known for their strange behavior. If an armadillo is startled, it will jump into the air. Sometimes it will even jump three feet high! It also makes a squealing sound. Armadillos are interesting animals!

STORY QUESTIONS

1. A good title for this reading passage would be . . .
   a. "The Armadillo State."
   b. "Locating an Armadillo."
   c. "The Basics of the Armadillo."
   d. "The Squeal of an Armadillo."

2. After reading the passage, what can you guess is one similarity between an armadillo and an anteater?
   a. They both live in Texas.
   b. They both eat ants.
   c. They both squeal.
   d. They both jump in the air when startled.

3. The author wrote this passage to . . .
   a. justify keeping armadillos in captivity.
   b. inform the reader of how armadillos are mistreated.
   c. share general information about armadillos.
   d. raise awareness of the shrinking armadillo population.

4. If you wanted to find out more about armadillos, you could . . .
   a. read a book about how armadillos dig their burrows.
   b. watch a television program about insects.
   c. meet somebody who lives in Texas.
   d. watch a television program about the different types of armadillo.

LLAMAS

Do you know what a llama is? Do you know how to say that word? A llama is an interesting animal. In English, the word is pronounced with the 'l' sound at the beginning (*lama*). In Spanish, the word is pronounced with a 'y' sound at the beginning (*yama*). The llama comes from South America. Llamas have been used as pack animals for thousands of years. They are strong and smart animals. They can hike on the toughest trails. The llama is able to carry over 200 pounds and can hike about 12 hours in a day. They are similar to camels and cows, in that they chew their own cud.

A llama can grow to be as big as 400 pounds. The life span of a llama is 15 to 29 years. Llamas come in a variety of colors. They can be brown, gray, black, or white, as well as a combination of colors. Llamas are herd animals and prefer to be with other llamas. Llamas are also known for spitting. They typically spit to show dominance to other llamas. They can see very well, and sometimes they are used to protect baby cows, sheep, or goats.

Llamas do make some noises. They can be heard humming, which sounds a lot like how you sound humming. They may also cluck or make an alarm sound. They use the alarm sound when they feel threatened or afraid. Llamas are also known to roll on the ground to fluff their wool. They prefer to roll in the dirt.

STORY QUESTIONS

1. What is this passage mainly about?
   a. how the llama eats
   b. predators of the llama
   c. the different types of llama
   d. general facts about the llama

2. In the second paragraph, what does the word *dominance* mean?
   a. supremacy
   b. broken
   c. structured
   d. overcome

3. Llamas are social animals and prefer to . . .
   a. hunt other animals.
   b. protect other animals.
   c. live in groups.
   d. roll on their backs.

4. Based on information in the passage, why are llamas good pack animals?
   a. They stay in groups.
   b. They are black and white.
   c. They are smaller than camels.
   d. They can carry a lot of weight.

SHARKS

Mention the word *shark* to someone on the beach and you are bound to get a reaction. Sharks have been the most feared predator of the ocean. Sharks are fish. They have been around since the time of dinosaurs. They can be found in oceans all over the world, and they have also been found in some rivers and lakes.

One difference between most other fish and a shark is that most fish have bones and a shark has cartilage. Cartilage is tough, but it is not as strong as bone. Another difference is that the shark is only able to swim forward, while most fish can swim forwards and backwards. Fish also generally have slippery scales, while a shark has rough scales that feel like sandpaper.

There are many different types of shark. In fact, there are about 368 different types. The differences include color, habitat, behavior, and size. Sharks are also known for their very sharp teeth. They do not use their teeth to chew their food. Instead they swallow large chunks of food. They have five rows of teeth. If a tooth is broken, it is replaced by another tooth.

Sharks are carnivores, meaning that they eat meat. Sharks do not normally attack people. It seems like sharks attack people a lot, but the chances of getting stung by a bee or getting hit by lightning are greater. Even so, experts say it is important to keep an eye out for sharks when swimming in the ocean.

STORY QUESTIONS

1. Sharks are greatly feared by humans because they . . .
   a. are good swimmers.
   b. are the right size.
   c. are carnivores.
   d. eat only plants.

2. According to the passage, how are sharks different from most other fish?
   a. They do not have scales.
   b. They are camouflaged
   c. They are slow moving.
   d. They are not able to swim backwards.

3. Why did the author include the first paragraph?
   a. to generally introduce sharks
   b. to clear up misconceptions about sharks
   c. to generate questions about sharks
   d. to identify the food eaten by sharks

4. The best way to find the answer to the previous question is to . . .
   a. reread the entire passage.
   b. reread the first paragraph and determine the main idea.
   c. look for the words *shark* and *habitat*.
   d. reread the fourth paragraph and determine the main idea.

Name _____ Date _____

THE ELEPHANT

Did you know that there are two different types of elephants? There is the African elephant and the Asian elephant. African elephants are the biggest land animals, and Asian elephants are the next biggest. Elephants are very social animals and live in groups. Female elephants head the groups. Only occasionally will a male elephant take charge of a group.

It's hard to imagine, but elephants are very good swimmers. This seems unusual because elephants are such big animals. Elephants can get as big as 10 feet tall and weigh about 6 tons! Male elephants are usually bigger than females. They have gray or brownish wrinkled skin that has almost no hair. Elephants are also known for their big ears. They can hear very well with these ears. These ears also help the elephant cool off.

The elephant breathes through the nostrils at the end of its very long trunk. The trunk is also used to get water and food. The elephant uses its trunk to suck up the water that is then shot into its mouth. The trunk also gathers food and brings it to the mouth. Elephants use their trunks similarly to the way that we use our hands. Elephants are herbivores, eating mostly roots, grasses, leaves, fruit, and tree bark. They use their tusks along with their trunks to get their food.

STORY QUESTIONS

1. How does the author feel about elephants?
   a. The author is in favor of elephant control.
   b. The author feels that elephants are interesting animals.
   c. The author is afraid of elephants.
   d. The author sees the need and purpose for more laws on elephant poaching.

2. The second paragraph informs the reader about . . .
   a. the anatomy of the elephant.
   b. the diet of an elephant.
   c. the history of the elephant.
   d. the predator of the elephant.

3. What is the meaning of the word *herbivore*?
   a. meat eater   c. plant eater
   b. meat or plant eater   d. none of the above

4. Where might this information about the elephant most likely be found?
   a. in a pamphlet on elephants
   b. in a newspaper article
   c. in a book about carnivores
   d. in a book about animals in Asia

THE BOA CONSTRICTOR

The boa constrictor is a large snake living in Central and South America. This large snake lives alone. Some people keep boas in the home to hunt rats. The boa constrictor is an endangered, protected animal.

Boa constrictors are carnivores, which means that they eat meat. They are mostly nocturnal animals, hunting at night. A boa constrictor does not bite its prey; it actually squeezes its prey to death. The boa then swallows its prey whole, usually head first, and lets the food digest inside its stomach. The stomach has very strong acids that digest the food. Boa constrictors have been known to eat small mammals, birds, and other reptiles. Once the boa has eaten, it does not need to eat for a few weeks. It takes that long to digest all the food!

Boa constrictors are cold-blooded animals. This means that they assume approximately the same temperature as their environment. They grow year after year to be one of the biggest snakes. They can get up to 10 feet long and weigh over 60 pounds. They are typically colored brown, black, or tan and come in a variety of patterns.

STORY QUESTIONS

1. Where in the passage would you find out what the boa constrictor eats?
   a. end of the first paragraph
   b. middle of the third paragraph
   c. end of the second paragraph
   d. the title

2. What does the boa constrictor have that helps it digest its food?
   a. claw-like teeth   c. strong muscles
   b. wings   d. stomach acids

3. The writer probably wrote this passage to . . .
   a. warn humans about the boa constrictor.
   b. enlighten farmers to the benefits of boa constrictors.
   c. determine the genealogy of the boa constrictor.
   d. inform the reader about the boa constrictor.

4. Which of the following is <u>not</u> a fact about the boa constrictor?
   a. The boa constrictor can weigh over 60 pounds.
   b. The boa constrictor does not chew its food.
   c. The boa constrictor is green in color.
   d. The boa constrictor can get up to 10 feet long.

DAILY Warm-Up 7   Name _____   Date _____

PENGUINS

The penguin is a fascinating bird. There are 17 different kinds of penguin. The penguin spends much of its life in the sea, so it can swim very well. A penguin is one of the few birds that cannot fly. A penguin uses its feathers to keep its skin dry. Its feathers are shiny and waterproof. Penguins continually lose their feathers and grow new ones. Penguins have big heads with short, thick necks. They have web-shaped feet for swimming and flipper-like wings for "gliding" through the water. Their coloring is usually black and white, although there are some brown penguins. Penguins are known for their "tuxedo" look.

The largest of the penguins is called the emperor penguin. This penguin stands at over three-and-a-half feet tall and weighs about 65 pounds. It is hard to tell the difference between male and female penguins because they look so much alike.

All wild penguins are found in the southern hemisphere. They live in climates ranging from warm tropics to very cold and frigid landscapes. Only penguins with a heavy amount of blubber can live in freezing climates. A penguin is not able to defend itself, so it lives in an area that is generally free from predators. Penguins eat fish, squid, and crustaceans.

Penguins are very social animals and have been known to mate with just one penguin during the breeding season. It is the female penguin that competes for a mate's attention.

STORY QUESTIONS

1. What does the author think of penguins?
   a. The author does not think highly of the penguins.
   b. The author thinks that penguins should not be classified as birds.
   c. The author thinks penguins live in groups.
   d. The author thinks the penguin is an interesting bird.

2. According to the passage, which sentence shows what the author thinks of the penguin?
   a. "Penguins are known for their 'tuxedo' look."
   b. "A penguin is one of the few birds that cannot fly."
   c. "The penguin is a fascinating bird."
   d. "It is hard to tell the difference between male and female penguins."

3. Why would a penguin with little blubber not be found in a freezing climate like Antarctica?
   a. It has too much blubber for such a cold place.
   b. It would get too warm.
   c. All penguins live in warm tropic climates.
   d. It does not have enough blubber to stay warm.

4. The penguin uses its feathers to . . .
   a. fly.   c. stay dry.
   b. stay warm.   d. move around.

ZEBRAS

The zebra is closely related to the donkey and the horse. They look very similar, except for the striking colors of the zebra. The zebra has very distinctive white stripes on a dark background. The dark color can be either black or dark brown. No two zebras have the same stripe pattern. The stripes on the zebra can help the zebra get away from its predators. The stripes make it difficult for the predator to judge distances. The zebra runs very fast, going as fast as 40 mph in no time at all. This quick speed enables the zebra to escape from predators easily.

Zebras live together in groups of up to 17. The stallions, or the males, stand at the back of the group to protect the young and the old zebras from predators. The dominant female leads the group. The zebras roam around looking for food. They are nomads. They eat grasses and stay close to water so that they have a water supply. A zebra can live to be up to 45 years old.

Zebras are most active in the early morning and in the late afternoon. They spend half of their waking hours eating. Zebras are hunted for their striking skins. They are also endangered because more and more of their grazing land is being replaced with farming land.

STORY QUESTIONS

1. What is the purpose of the stripes on the zebra?
   a. to stabilize the zebra
   b. a characteristic used to identify the difference between zebra species
   c. to help the zebra protect itself
   d. to aid the zebra in gathering food

2. Identify a supporting detail that explains the statement, "The stripes on the zebra can help the zebra get away from its predators."
   a. Zebras are hunted for their striking skins.
   b. The stripes make it difficult for the predator to judge distances.
   c. The zebras live in groups of up to seventeen.
   d. A zebra can live to be up to 45 years old.

3. After reading the passage, which question could you answer about the zebra?
   a. How does the zebra protect itself?
   b. How many different types of zebras are there?
   c. How does the zebra get the stripes on its skin?
   d. How does the mother zebra feed its young?

THE ANTELOPE

An antelope is a hoofed animal with horns that are hollow. There are many different kinds of antelope. Antelope live in the mountains, deserts, and wetlands and are hunted by lions, hyenas, and other carnivores. They are light, quick-moving animals that can jump very well. Some antelopes can reach speeds as fast as 60 mph. They can bounce on all four legs. This is called *pronking*.

Antelopes feed on grass, desert plants, and young plant shoots. They also eat twigs and leaves. They swallow the food whole and then regurgitate it and chew it. This is called cud. Most antelopes live in Africa but have also been found in Asia and North America. Antelopes come in all different colors and sizes. The horns of antelope can be curved or straight. These horns never fall off and are used to get food.

An antelope has very keen senses. They have big eyes and keen hearing. This helps the antelope stay on constant alert for predators that may be nearby.

STORY QUESTIONS

1. Which of the following sentences is factual, based on information from the passage?
   a. Antelopes come in a variety of shapes and sizes.
   b. Unfortunately, there are no current laws protecting the antelope.
   c. The antelope has such an interesting coat.
   d. The tails of an antelope help them run fast.

2. According to this passage, antelopes are . . .
   a. carnivores.   c. both carnivores and herbivores.
   b. herbivores.   d. none of the above.

3. You can conclude that an antelope would probably do well living in all of these places *except* the . . .
   a. desert.
   b. mountain ranges.
   c. ocean.
   d. Everglades.

4. Where might this information about the antelope be found?
   a. in a fashion magazine
   b. in a newspaper article
   c. in a book about herbivores
   d. in a book about animals in Australia

THE KOALA

Have you ever seen a cute and cuddly koala? These animals look an awful lot like teddy bears, but they are not bears. A full-grown koala gets about as big as a yardstick and can weigh up to 20 pounds. Koalas have a very specific diet. They eat only the leaves from a eucalyptus tree. They eat as much as two-and-a-half pounds of eucalyptus leaves a day. Koalas enjoy the moist and tender tips of these leaves. The koala is able to get enough water and food from the leaves.

Koalas have large, bushy ears with small, beady eyes. They have a baby-like expression, which makes them look cute to humans. Their four paws are sharp so that they can easily climb trees. They have a thick, soft, gray or brown fur. Koalas are also good swimmers.

A baby koala stays in its mother's pouch for about six months before it learns to feed by itself. Koalas primarily come from Australia. Many koalas prefer to live on the island on the southeast shore of Australia. Koalas are becoming endangered because their habitat is being destroyed due to construction. Some are also killed for their skins. The main predators of a baby koala are eagles and owls. Humans and dingoes, Australian wild dogs, also kill them. If a koala spots an enemy, it will scurry up a tree for safety.

STORY QUESTIONS

1. In this passage, the word *specific* means . . .
   a. order.
   b. exact.
   c. categorize.
   d. patronize.

2. Which statement is false?
   a. The koala carries its baby in a pouch for six months.
   b. The koala eats eucalyptus leaves.
   c. The koala has to live near a watering hole.
   d. The koala has sharp claws.

3. According to the passage, why do koalas seem so cute to humans?
   a. because of the hair on their ears
   b. because of their black, beady eyes
   c. because of their baby-like expression
   d. because they can scurry quickly up a tree

THE RIVER OTTER

What animal has a sleek, furry body and swims in the river? That would be the river otter. The thick, dense fur helps the otter keep warm in the cold water. The river otter is a type of weasel. The river otter can be found in lakes, rivers, streams, marshes, and ponds. They are found predominantly in Canada and the United States. The river otter is an endangered animal because hunters desire their furry skins.

River otters are nocturnal animals, which means they do most of their activities at night. They hunt and fish at night and sleep during the day. River otters live in dens dug under the ground. They usually take over old dens from other animals, such as beavers. The bear, coyote, and the bald eagle are all predators of the river otter.

The river otter is a carnivore, which means that it eats meat. Its diet consists of crustaceans, fish, small mammals, birds, insects, and amphibians. Sea otters have a very strong sense of smell. They also use their whiskers to help them find food. Like sea otters, river otters are also known for their ability to play. They can do somersaults, sliding, wrestling, and even belly flops. They love to slide down a muddy or snowy hill. River otters use their webbed feet to swim around in the water, and they can stay underwater for up to four minutes.

STORY QUESTIONS

1. Which of the following statements is <u>not</u> true about the river otter?
   a. The river otter's fur helps it withstand the extreme temperatures of the water.
   b. The webbed feet help the river otter swim in the water.
   c. The river otter lays its eggs along the riverbank.
   d. The river otter uses its whiskers to locate prey.

2. The word *predator* used in this passage means . . .
   a. similar.
   b. hunter.
   c. amicable.
   d. carnivore.

3. Which of the following is <u>not</u> a benefit of thick, dense fur?
   a. It prevents the river otter from getting cold.
   b. It helps the otter move quickly.
   c. It stores food.
   d. It serves as protection.

4. A synonym for *dense* as used in the first paragraph is . . .
   a. heavy.
   b. transparent.
   c. bristle.
   d. endangered.

THE COTTONTAIL RABBIT

The cottontail rabbit gets its name because its tail looks like a ball of cotton. The color of the cottontail rabbit is reddish brown with a white tail. The adult grows to be about 12 to 18 inches long and weighs anywhere from two to four pounds. The cottontail rabbit likes to live in the brush in order to hide. It makes its home in a burrow near prickly bushes. This rabbit is unaffected by the prickly bushes, but living near these prickly bushes deters some predators from attacking the rabbit. Coyotes, red foxes, hawks, and owls are all predators of the cottontail rabbit.

A cottontail will have multiple litters of babies each year. It is not uncommon for a rabbit to have many babies. The babies are born without fur and they cannot see. After about a week, the fur begins to grow in. The mother rabbit builds a nest out of grass, fur, and hay to keep the babies warm.

This rabbit is an herbivore, eating grass, bark, berries, twigs, and just about anything that is green. If a cottontail is lucky enough to come across a farmer's garden, it will eat just about any vegetables growing. They especially like carrots, potatoes, and tomatoes.

Famous stories have been written about cottontail rabbits. Perhaps you've heard one about Peter and his sisters Flopsy, Mopsy, and Cottontail.

STORY QUESTIONS

1. When do you think a cottontail rabbit would leave its home in the brush?
   a. to seek food
   b. to seek safety
   c. to chase away its enemy
   d. to seek protection

2. Which of the following statements is true?
   a. The cottontail rabbit does not jump very well.
   b. The cottontail rabbit is a carnivore.
   c. Most of the animals that eat rabbit eat the red fox, as well.
   d. Cottontail rabbits have a tail like a ball of cotton.

3. In this passage, the word *unaffected* means . . .
   a. unchanged.
   b. unharmed.
   c. killed instantly.
   d. unchallenged.

THE RED FOX

The red fox is a rusty red color with a whitish color on the belly. This animal is about the same size as a dog. The ears on a red fox are prominent, which make it look much different than a dog. The tail is bushy with a white tip. Other color varieties of the red fox also occur, including black, silver, and a cross phase in which a dark area crosses over the shoulders and down the middle of the back. The red fox prefers to roam where there is a marsh and field or along the edge of the forest. It can also be found on farmland, prairies, and in woodlands. The red fox thrives in British Columbia.

The red fox has a great sense of smell, hearing, and sight. This makes it a great predator. It can track and catch prey quickly and easily. The fox is an omnivore, which means it eats both meat and plants. The fox feeds on berries, grasses, apples, birds, small animals, insects, and corn. The enemies of the red fox are the coyote, the lynx, and humans. Humans are sometimes quick to kill a fox if it is seen on their property.

The red fox grows to be about three-and-a-half feet long and weighs between 10 and 15 pounds. It has long legs and it has a body built for speed. It has a long nose, erect ears, and narrow eyes. The red fox is most active at night. It may spend more time awake during the day in the winter because food is scarce then.

STORY QUESTIONS

1. A likely reason people might think the red fox is cunning and crafty is because of its . . .
   a. ability to run fast.
   b. big size.
   c. smell.
   d. look.

2. Another word for *prey* is . . .
   a. prayer.
   b. characteristic.
   c. victim.
   d. diet.

3. Which of the following would be the most accurate description of the red fox's diet?
   a. vegetables and corn
   b. berries, grasses, apples, birds, small animals, insects, and corn
   c. small animals, insects, and corn
   d. berries, grasses, apples, birds, coyotes, insects, and corn

4. The red fox has keen senses of . . .
   a. taste, smell, and hearing.
   b. hearing, sight, and touch.
   c. sight, hearing, and smell.
   d. smell, sight, and taste.

THE CRAB SPIDER

The crab spider is an interesting spider. It matches the color of the flower it lives on. This helps it stay camouflaged and hide from other insects. It takes this spider three days to change colors to match its environment. The crab spider pounces on any unsuspecting insects as soon as they land on the flower it's on. The spider bites the insects with its fangs and paralyzes them. The crab spider sucks up all the body fluids and leaves an empty husk.

Crab spiders do not spin webs. They spin fluffy silk cocoons to protect their eggs. The female spider can lay up to 20 to 30 eggs at a time. The spiderlings climb out of the cocoon after they shed their skin. Crab spiders live for one year.

The crab spider's body is divided into two parts with a narrow waist in the middle. The front legs are longer and thicker than the other legs so that they can hold their prey. They have a huge abdomen with simple black eyes that don't see very well. The spider gets its name because it walks sideways like a crab. This spider spends most of its time crouched in tree trunks, flowers, or leaves.

STORY QUESTIONS

1. How did the crab spider get its name?
   a. from its spotted back
   b. from the sound it makes
   c. from the way it walks
   d. from the manner in which it eats

2. What is the meaning of the word *pounced* as used in this passage?
   a. swooped
   b. leaped
   c. jumped
   d. attacked suddenly

3. How is the crab spider different from other spiders?
   a. It fights gravity.
   b. It emits a powerful force on its prey.
   c. It emits an odor in defense.
   d. It lives on a flower instead of a web.

4. Which of the following statements about the crab spider is true?
   a. The crab spider eats other spiders.
   b. The crab spider takes three days to change color.
   c. The crab spider spins a very sticky web.
   d. The body of the crab spider is divided into three parts.

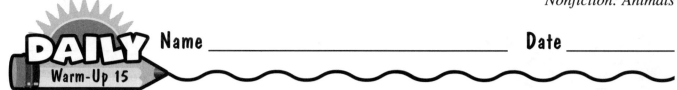

HARVEST MICE

Harvest mice are graceful animals. They climb from one plant to another with great ease. Each resembles a monkey swinging on the branches of a tree through the forest. These mice scamper through the forest looking for food. They feed on seeds and insects. They have to eat a lot of food in the summertime so that they can store enough food energy as fat for the winter months. This is necessary so they can stay in shelter from the cold. In the winter, the harvest mouse leaves the nest only during the warmest hours of the day.

The harvest mouse has a very long tail. The tail is helpful and works a lot like another hand or foot. It grabs onto the grass and supports the mouse. It also helps the mouse hang upside down and balance itself when it climbs upwards.

Harvest mice are some of the smallest mice in the world. An adult male harvest mouse weighs less than one-third of an ounce and measures no more than six inches—and that includes the tail! Harvest mice make a shrieking sound, and some of their noises are too high-pitched for humans to hear. These shrieks are usually a sign of distress.

STORY QUESTIONS

1. Why does the author say that harvest mice are graceful animals?
   a. Harvest mice make a shrieking sound.
   b. The harvest mouse has a very long tail.
   c. They climb from one plant to another with ease.
   d. They have to eat a lot of food in the summertime.

2. What is the topic of the second paragraph?
   a. the diet of the harvest mouse
   b. the enemies of the harvest mouse
   c. the color of the harvest mouse
   d. the tail of the harvest mouse

3. What is the meaning of the word *scamper* as used in the first paragraph?
   a. settle
   b. jump
   c. retrieve
   d. scurry

4. Which paragraph explains the noises a harvest mouse makes?
   a. first
   b. second
   c. third
   d. not in the passage

THE SEA ANEMONE

The sea anemone is closely related to the coral and the jellyfish. It looks a lot like a flower called the anemone, which is how it got its name. The animal's body has a plant-like appearance. It comes in a variety of colors, including red, blue, pink, and green. The sea anemone is an invertebrate, which means it has no skeleton. This sea animal attaches itself to rocks, the sea floor, coral, or other firm objects.

The sea anemone is a predatory animal that stings its prey with its tentacles. This paralyzes the victim, and the sea anemone then pushes the animal into the mouth. The sea anemone eats small fish, worms, mussels, and zooplankton. Very few animals eat the sea anemone. The great sea slug is one of its predators.

The sea anemone can grow up to 10 inches wide. It has a long, hollow tube. It likes to live in dark places and in warm waters. The sea anemone has an interesting relationship with other sea animals. The hermit crab places the sea anemone on top of its shell to use it as camouflage. The clown fish lives amongst the sea anemone for protection. The clown fish is not affected by the sea anemone's stinging tentacles. For most fish, though, avoiding the sea anemone is the best option.

STORY QUESTIONS

1. What would be a good title for this reading passage?
   a. "The Sea Anemone's Diet"
   b. "The Anemone's Habitat"
   c. "Interesting Facts and Details about the Sea Anemone"
   d. "Indigenous Animals of the Sea"

2. Which paragraph explains the eating habits of the sea anemone?
   a. first
   b. second
   c. third
   d. not mentioned in passage

3. Locate the statement below that is a fact.
   a. The sea anemone is a colorful ocean plant.
   b. The sea anemone is a nocturnal animal.
   c. The sea anemone has short legs.
   d. The sea anemone attaches itself to rocks and other firm surfaces.

4. In this passage, the word *predatory* means . . .
   a. prays often.
   b. using one's nose to locate things.
   c. digging in the ocean floor.
   d. killing for food.

ANNE SULLIVAN

Anne Sullivan was born on April 14, 1866, in Feeding Hills, Massachusetts. She was born to Irish immigrant farmers. She had one brother, Jimmie, who was crippled from tuberculosis. Anne's family was extremely poor, and her father was an alcoholic and abusive. When she was five years old, Anne got a serious eye infection that left her almost completely blind. Her mother died two years later, and her father put both of the children in an orphanage. Her brother died shortly after being placed in the orphanage.

When the head of the orphanage came to visit, Anne pleaded and begged him to let her go to school. She was allowed to go to school, and after a few operations, she regained some of her vision and managed to graduate at the top of her class from the Perkins Institute for the Blind.

Anne began some of her most important work when she was called on to tutor a young blind and deaf girl named Helen Keller. Helen was seven years old and very undisciplined. Anne had to teach her obedience before anything else. A breakthrough finally happened, and Anne was able to teach Helen to read words using Braille and the manual alphabet. Anne helped Helen go on to accomplish great things. Both Anne and Helen were invited to make speeches all over the world. Anne's work had a lasting impact on Helen and others, including both blind and sighted people. She continues to be an inspiration.

STORY QUESTIONS

1. What are the author's feelings about Anne Sullivan?
   a. indifferent
   b. disapproves
   c. unsure
   d. approves

2. Which sentence shows how the author feels about Anne Sullivan?
   a. She managed to graduate at the top of her class from the Perkins Institute.
   b. She continues to be an inspiration.
   c. Despite all of her struggles, Anne worked hard to succeed.
   d. Anne's family was extremely poor and her father was an alcoholic and abusive.

3. Which sentence is not an example of the Anne's accomplishments?
   a. Anne began some of her most important work when she was called on to tutor a young blind and deaf girl named Helen Keller.
   b. Anne had to teach her obedience before anything else.
   c. Anne helped Helen go on to accomplish great things.
   d. Her mother died two years later, and her father put both of the children in an orphanage.

ALBERT EINSTEIN

Albert Einstein was born in Ulm, Germany, in 1879. As a young boy, Einstein lived in Munich and Milan. At the age of five, his father showed him a compass and explained how it worked. Albert was intrigued with the idea that something in "space" made the needle work. At this time, Albert's mother also insisted that he learn to play the violin.

Albert was not considered very bright in school, and some even thought he had dyslexia and other learning problems. Many thought he was very slow. Nonetheless, school would go on to be very important to Albert, and he would go on to become a professor.

He eventually went to school in Switzerland, where he graduated from the Federal Institute of Technology. He then worked in a patent office and on his doctorate degree. He later became a professor of physics. Einstein developed the theory of relativity and received a Nobel Prize in physics in 1921. He became famous throughout the world, which is very unusual for a scientist.

STORY QUESTIONS

1. Why was Albert Einstein so successful in his life?
   a. People felt sorry for him and took pity on him.
   b. He did not let what other people thought of him get him down.
   c. He learned to say no when it was most important.
   d. He was able to become famous worldwide.

2. What can you learn about Albert Einstein from reading this passage?
   a. He was curious.
   b. He was very learning disabled.
   c. He was denied U.S. citizenship.
   d. He was placed in an orphanage.

3. Which of the following statements is true, based on information in the passage?
   a. Albert Einstein flunked out of his school.
   b. Albert Einstein refused to play the violin.
   c. Albert Einstein was given the Nobel Prize.
   d. Young scientists began writing letters to Albert Einstein.

4. Which of the following would make a great title for this passage?
   a. "The Theory of Relativity"
   b. "Albert Einstein vs. The Scientific World"
   c. "Einstein's Education"
   d. "A Brief Story of Albert Einstein"

FRANKLIN D. ROOSEVELT

On January 30, 1882, Franklin D. Roosevelt (F.D.R.) was born. He would go on to become the 32nd president of the United States. At an early age, he was taught by his parents and private tutors. In 1896, he attended a prep school. He went to college to study history and the law.

F.D.R. married his cousin, Anna Eleanor Roosevelt. Together they had six children. Five of them lived. By this time, Franklin was very involved in politics and was reelected to the state senate of New York. He became more and more involved in politics. He was nominated as vice president, but he did not win the election and went back to private life.

While vacationing on Campobello Island, Franklin became sick with polio. This disease took away the use of his legs, and he would never walk after that. Eleanor encouraged him and supported him in his efforts to enter politics again. This time he became governor of New York. After being reelected, Franklin ran for president.

F.D.R. was sworn in as president in January 1933. While president, he worked hard to help overcome the Great Depression. He also led the U.S. into the Second World War. Eleanor was a great support to Franklin. She also played a great role as first lady of the United States.

STORY QUESTIONS

1. What does the word *nominated* mean in this passage?
   a. requested
   b. selected
   c. ordered
   d. pushed

2. After reading the passage, what is a word that could be used to describe F.D.R.?
   a. studious
   b. talented
   c. rugged
   d. determined

3. F.D.R.'s time as president could be described as . . .
   a. successful and accomplished.
   b. supportive yet unsuccessful.
   c. typical and normal.
   d. unhappy and unsettled.

LOUISA MAY ALCOTT

Born in 1832 the second of four daughters to Amos and Abigail Alcott, Louisa was known to have a very bad temper. Her family struggled financially. Her mother had to work hard because her father had a hard time maintaining a job. As a child, Louisa and her sisters had grand imaginations. They would make up stories and plays. They pretended to be fairies in the woods.

Louisa began writing to try to bring in money for the family. Her first poem was published in *Peterson's Magazine*. It didn't bring in a lot of money, but it gave Louisa a lot of confidence. She served as a nurse to wounded soldiers in World War I until she became ill. She almost died before she miraculously recovered. Louisa struggled with illness the rest of her life.

Louisa is best known for *Little Women*, a book that received immediate success. The book was based on Louisa's life with her family. This book helped Louisa become an established author. She would go on to write other books, such as *Good Wives, Little Men*, and many more. The books *Little Women* and *Little Men* have been made into plays, as well as movies.

STORY QUESTIONS

1. What type of book was *Little Women*?
   a. poetry
   b. novel
   c. set of short stories
   d. mystery

2. Louisa began writing as a means to . . .
   a. be trained as an author.
   b. teach others how to write.
   c. earn money for the family.
   d. learn about the publishing world.

3. What is the meaning of the word *established* as used in the last paragraph?
   a. enforced
   b. recognized
   c. instructed
   d. enjoyed

4. What is the main idea of paragraph three?
   a. to introduce Louisa's background
   b. to mention some of the books Louisa wrote
   c. to learn about Louisa's sisters
   d. to compare the real life family with the account in *Little Women*

LOUIS BRAILLE

A young French boy invented the Braille system of reading at the age of 12. This form of reading was different than any other. It changed words into raised dots in different combinations. The Braille system enabled blind people to finally read. Louis himself was blind.

Louis was born near Paris on January 4, 1809. He became blind by accident. When he was only three years old, he grabbed an awl. An awl is a tool used to make holes. The awl slipped and hurt his eye. His eye was infected, and soon the other eye became infected. Louis lost sight in both eyes. It was very difficult for Louis, but soon he learned to adjust to his blindness. He began looking for ways to continue learning. He went to a special school for the blind.

While there, he began creating an alphabet based on an old army code. It consisted of raised bumps and slashes, but it was a long process. When Louis arrived home on vacation, he began experimenting with a dull awl making bumps on paper. Each letter of the alphabet consisted of six dots arranged differently. This would make reading much faster and easier for a blind person. Louis Braille used the same tool that caused his blindness to help blind people to read! It was an amazing achievement.

STORY QUESTIONS

1. Which of the following statements could be made about Louis Braille?
   a. Louis learned to write books using the Braille system.
   b. Louis's accident ended up improving the lives of blind people everywhere.
   c. Louis Braille could have used more support from his parents.
   d. Louis Braille used his anger to improve his life.

2. What conclusions can be drawn about Louis Braille after reading this passage?
   a. He was religious and dedicated to missionary work.
   b. He was wealthy and lived a life of luxury.
   c. He was hard-working and persevering.
   d. He was lazy and undetermined.

3. Which statement explains why Louis Braille's system was successful?
   a. He began looking for ways to continue learning.
   b. Each letter of the alphabet consisted of six dots arranged differently.
   c. This would make reading much faster and easier for a blind person.
   d. It was an amazing discovery.

4. What is the meaning of the word *enabled* as used in the passage?
   a. made possible
   b. injured
   c. unable
   d. judged

SACAGAWEA

Sacagawea was born in what is now the state of Idaho to a Shoshone chief.   She was kidnapped by the Hidatsa when she was about 10 years old. She and another girl were purchased by Charbonneau, a French Canadian trapper who married Sacagawea. The famous duo Lewis and Clark asked Charbonneau to serve as an interpreter on their historical expedition. He agreed but asked if Sacagawea could go with them.

Sacagawea turned out to be a great asset to the group. She helped with translation, and according to Clark she was a "token of peace" to the Indians they would meet. Sacagawea would have her first child on the trail. She would also meet up with her brother, who was head of the Shoshone tribe. It was an incredible reunion. She did not stay with her lost family but continued on with the expedition.

The history of what happened after the Lewis and Clark expedition ended is somewhat fuzzy. Some experts say that Sacagawea went with her husband to St. Louis at the invitation of Clark. She would later die of a fever. Other accounts say that she went back to the Shoshone tribe on the Wind River Reservation, where she died in 1884. Either way, Sacagawea was a great person in American history.

STORY QUESTIONS

1. What is meant by the word *asset* as used in the passage?
   a. money
   b. advantage
   c. weakness
   d. cook

2. What is the meaning of the phrase "token of peace"?
   a. They didn't have a dove so they used Sacagawea.
   b. If the Indians saw Sacagawea, they knew she would be on their side.
   c. When the Indians saw a female Indian, they would not think the men meant harm.
   d. Sacagawea would receive payment if she was able to interpret and interact peaceably with the Indians.

3. After reading the passage, what can you infer about Sacagawea on the Lewis and Clark expedition?
   a. She was a hard worker and able to handle the great strain of traveling.
   b. She was weak and needed a lot of support.
   c. She was able to find hope in her new life.
   d. She was defiant and stubborn.

4. Which statement explains what made Sacagawea so famous?
   a. She was the first Shoshone Indian to be kidnapped.
   b. She was the first female to travel to the Northwestern United States.
   c. She was able to serve as an interpreter and help to Lewis and Clark.
   d. She was able to speak nine languages.

Name _____

Date _____

FRANK SINATRA

Frank Sinatra, who many consider to be one of the greatest singers of all time, never had plans to become a singer. Born on December 12, 1915, Frank grew up wanting to be a sportswriter. He worked as an office boy for a local newspaper. But after hearing Bing Crosby and Billie Holiday, he began singing. He got a quartet together to sing, which led to a job as a singing waiter at a roadhouse. He got his big break in 1939. He joined the Harry James band and sang famous songs like "From the Bottom of My Heart."

Frank was soon lured away by Tommy Dorsey. Dorsey helped him to become a sensation throughout the 1940s. His crooning voice drove the audiences wild. The women loved his soft voice. Sinatra got a start in movies in the late 1940s and he would continue to star in films throughout the 1950s. His first film was *Las Vegas Nights*.

Frank would marry four times. His last wife, Barbara, was said to have a calming effect on him. He was known for his wild parties with the "Rat Pack," which included such famous figures as Dean Martin and Sammy Davis, Jr. At the age of 71, he was hospitalized to have surgery on his intestines. In March 1994, he was hospitalized again. Two years after that, he was in the hospital again for a pinched nerve. Two months later, he would die of a heart attack.

STORY QUESTIONS

1. A good title for this reading passage would be . . .
   a. "The Rat Pack"
   b. "Frank Sinatra: The Actor"
   c. "Life and Times of Frank Sinatra"
   d. "Frank and Family"

2. Which of the following statements about Frank Sinatra is true?
   a. He was hospitalized for a broken back.
   b. He wanted to be a sportswriter for the newspaper.
   c. He claimed ownership of the "Rat Pack."
   d. He was taught to sing by Sammy Davis, Jr.

3. In the second paragraph, what does the word *crooning* mean?
   a. soft, low tone
   b. high-pitched voice
   c. ear-splitting scream
   d. low baritone

4. Why was Frank Sinatra's singing so appreciated by the fans?
   a. He hypnotized the audiences.
   b. He was creative and young.
   c. He was able to sing in a crooning voice that audiences loved.
   d. He had been taught voice lessons by a great singer.

Name _____ **Date** _____

ELIZABETH CADY STANTON

Elizabeth Cady Stanton played a big role in the history of women's rights. She and her longtime colleague Susan B. Anthony remained friends to the end. Elizabeth was an active abolitionist, which meant that she was against slavery. She met and married her husband, Harry Stanton, in 1840. The two worked together to do away with slavery. They traveled to London for the World Anti-Slavery Convention. They were upset to find out that women were not allowed to be delegates.

Elizabeth came home to work on the issue of women's rights. This is when she met Susan B. Anthony. They worked as a team to help women gain more rights. Elizabeth played the role of writer, and Susan would set up the plans for the group. They worked to get women the right to vote. They were upset when only free men were given the right to vote after the Civil War. Elizabeth also worked to change the property laws for women. She also felt that women should be able to divorce if they were in abusive relationships.

Elizabeth would die on October 26, 1902. This was nearly 20 years before women were given the right to vote. Her home in Seneca Falls, New York, now has documents relating to Elizabeth's hard work and efforts for women on display. Her writings continue to inspire women today.

STORY QUESTIONS

1. Which sentence below shows Elizabeth's contributions to the women's rights movement?
   a. Elizabeth played the role of writer, and Susan would set up the plans for the movement.
   b. She met and married her husband Harry Stanton in 1840.
   c. The two worked together to do away with slavery.
   d. She died nearly 20 years before women were given the right to vote.

2. What is the main idea of the third paragraph?
   a. It introduces the main idea of the passage.
   b. It discusses Elizabeth's contributions to women's rights.
   c. It discusses Elizabeth's experiences as a writer.
   d. It explains the relationship between Susan B. Anthony and Elizabeth.

3. The best way to answer the previous question is to . . .
   a. reread the entire passage.
   b. reread the first paragraph.
   c. look for the words "rights" and "Elizabeth Stanton."
   d. reread the third paragraph and determine the main idea.

Name _____ Date _____

DANIEL BOONE

Daniel Boone was a great explorer of the frontier. He is given credit for settling the state of Kentucky. Born on November 2, 1734, to a weaver and a blacksmith, Boone was raised in Pennsylvania. His childhood was preparation for his adult life. He loved to make friends with the Indians and observe wildlife. At the age of 12, Daniel was given his first gun.

The family soon moved to North Carolina. It took a year for them to get there and get settled. Daniel would leave at 19 to fight in the French and Indian War. When he returned, he met a hunter named John Finley who told him stories about the frontier. This got Daniel thinking and dreaming. But he was not quite ready to explore. He married Rebecca Bryan.

In 1767, he traveled to the end of Kentucky. He was asked by Finley to explore even more country with his crew. It wasn't until two years later that he finally returned home. He had explored all over Kentucky. Daniel continued to explore for many more years. He eventually left Kentucky, saying that it was "too crowded." He died at the age of 85 and was buried next to his wife.

STORY QUESTIONS

1. The author feels that Daniel Boone was . . .
   a. intelligent and loved learning.
   b. motivated by money.
   c. interested in traveling the oceans.
   d. a great explorer in American history.

2. Which statement supports the author's opinion of Daniel Boone?
   a. Daniel continued to explore for many more years.
   b. Daniel Boone was a great explorer of the frontier.
   c. He had explored all over Kentucky.
   d. His childhood was preparation for his adult life.

3. The third paragraph informs the reader about . . .
   a. Daniel's early life in North Carolina.
   b. Daniel's travels across Kentucky.
   c. Daniel's desire to stay in Kentucky.
   d. Daniel's childhood in Pennsylvania.

4. Where else might this reading passage about Daniel Boone be found?
   a. in a book about the French and Indian War
   b. in a pamphlet about the great leaders of the United States
   c. on a website about the early explorers of the United States
   d. on a website about famous Indian traders of the United States

DAILY
Warm-Up 10

Name _____ Date _____

AMELIA EARHART

Do you love to fly in an airplane? Amelia Earhart sure did. This woman aviator took her first pilot lessons at the age of 23. On July 24, 1897, Amelia was born in her grandparents' home in Kansas. Her little sister was born two years later. Their grandparents had a lot of money, and so Amelia and her sister were sent to private schools and lived a privileged life. Their father, on the other hand, struggled to keep a job and eventually tore the family apart with his drinking. Her mother took the girls and moved to live with friends in Chicago.

Amelia went on to train as a nurse and served in the "Great War" as a volunteer nurse's aid. Afterwards, she enrolled as a pre-med student at Columbia University. It was in California that she first went to an "aerial meet." She boarded a plane that flew over Los Angeles. Amelia was in love. She couldn't get enough of flying.

This desire to fly encouraged her to take lessons from Anita Snook, and she bought her first plane. She began trying to break records. She was asked by George Putnam to try to be the first lady to fly across the Atlantic.

Many years later, Amelia had broken several records. She was the first woman to fly the Atlantic solo and the only person to fly it twice. She also flew the longest non-stop distance flown by a woman and set another record for crossing in the shortest time.

STORY QUESTIONS

1. Where would you read to find out about Amelia's first introduction to flying a plane?
   a. first paragraph
   b. second paragraph
   c. third paragraph
   d. fourth paragraph

2. The author probably wrote this passage to . . .
   a. warn readers about the dangers of flying.
   b. inform readers about Amelia's weaknesses.
   c. inform readers of Amelia's record-setting history.
   d. inform readers of Amelia's experience with George Putnam.

3. How many records did Amelia set which are listed in this passage?
   a. one   c. six
   b. three   d. four

4. Which of the following statements is <u>not</u> a fact about Amelia Earhart?
   a. Amelia loved to fly airplanes.
   b. Amelia was born in Kansas.
   c. Amelia grew up flying airplanes.
   d. Amelia went to private school.

JACKIE ROBINSON

Though he was born in Cairo, Georgia, in 1919, Jackie Robinson grew up in Los Angeles, California. Although African-American athletes were not accepted in all sports leagues at this time, Jackie's life would prove that athletes should be judged by their abilities and not by the color of their skin. Jackie would prove to be a star athlete. He was a star in not just one sport, but four: he ran track and played basketball, football, and baseball. Jackie began playing professional baseball in the Negro American Baseball League. But after two years, he joined the Brooklyn Dodgers. No other African-American had ever been allowed to play in the major leagues.

Not everyone thought that an African-American person should play in the major leagues. The fans and some of the other players treated Jackie very poorly. They were trying to get him to leave the league. The opposite happened: Jackie only worked harder and played harder. He managed to win the Rookie of the Year award and helped the Dodgers win the pennant. In 1949, he had the best batting average in the league and won the Most Valuable Player award.

Jackie continued to work hard and improve. He was also an excellent fielder and base runner. In the 10 years that Jackie played for the Dodgers, they won the pennant six times and the World Series championship once. In 1962, Jackie Robinson was elected to the Baseball Hall of Fame.

STORY QUESTIONS

1. Where would you read to find out about Jackie's experiences playing for the Dodgers?
   a. end of the first paragraph
   b. in the second paragraph
   c. end of the third paragraph
   d. second and third paragraphs

2. The author probably wrote this passage to . . .
   a. inform the reader of the civil rights for all Americans.
   b. inform the reader about Jackie's time as a batter.
   c. inform the reader about Jackie's great accomplishments.
   d. portray Jackie's commitment to helping others learn to play baseball.

3. What does the word *average* mean in this passage?
   a. score in a baseball game
   b. opening
   c. level
   d. percentage

4. Which of the following statements is <u>not</u> a fact about Jackie Robinson?
   a. Jackie was successful because of hard work and determination.
   b. Jackie let the fans and other players run him out of baseball.
   c. Jackie was elected to the Hall of Fame.
   d. Jackie played for the Brooklyn Dodgers.

DAILY Warm-Up 12

Name _____ Date _____

LANGSTON HUGHES

Langston Hughes was a famous poet and writer in the early 1930s. He became famous and was known as the voice of black people. The subject of all of his writing was about the lives of African Americans. Born in Joplin, Missouri, his family eventually moved to Ohio. He began writing poetry in eigth grade. Upon graduation from high school, he was voted the class poet.

By the age of 18, Langston saw his first poem published. The title of the poem was "The Negro Speaks of Rivers." For a short while, he attended Columbia University. He decided to make a trip to Africa. He boarded a ship and traveled to many countries in Africa and Europe. He would later go on to get a college degree.

One of his favorite things to do was to listen to jazz and blues music. This influence of music began to appear in his writing. He moved to Harlem, where he was editor. He devoted a great portion of his life to writing and speaking.

He wrote over 16 poetry books, two novels, and 20 plays, as well as children's poetry, musicals, operas, biographies, radio and television scripts, and dozens of magazine articles. He was able to influence many people with his writing

STORY QUESTIONS

1. Based on the passage, what were some of Langston Hughes's writing interests?
   a. writing about slavery
   b. writing about the lives of black people, jazz, and blues
   c. writing about being the first black poet
   d. writing about experiences in foreign countries

2. After reading the passage, why do you think Langston wanted to travel to Africa?
   a. He wanted to look up his ancestors.
   b. He wanted to travel the world.
   c. He wanted to see what life was like in Africa.
   d. He was given free voyage and he didn't want to pass up the opportunity.

3. What is the main idea of the passage?
   a. Through hard work and dedication, Langston was able to get African-Americans the right to vote.
   b. Work before play is a good motto to live by.
   c. Langston owed his life to the community in which he was raised.
   d. Langston was able to portray African-American life, and he was able to help give African-Americans voice.

Name _____   Date _____

ANNE FRANK

Anne Frank was a young girl who wrote a diary that has probably been read by more people than any other diary. Anne was born on June 12, 1929, in Germany. She lived during the time that Adolf Hitler was taking over Eastern Europe and exterminating the Jews and other non-Aryans who lived there. Her family escaped to the Netherlands, where they thought they would be safe. But Hitler and his armies eventually came to the Netherlands and attempted to round up all of the Jews.

Because of the kindness of friends, Anne's family was taken to an empty section of her father's office building, where they were hidden for almost two years. Anne had received a diary that she lovingly called Kitty. She wrote in her diary on a regular basis. This diary shared with the world what life was like living in this hiding place.

On August 4, 1944, the Frank family was betrayed. Someone told the German officers of the family living in the hiding place, and they were found. The family was sent to work in a camp. Anne and her sister, Margot, had to smash batteries. The acid burned the girls' skin. Anne and her sister would die of typhus just weeks before the British army liberated the camp.

Anne's diary was found by some of the workers in the building where they hid. The diary was published in 1947. The diary has been translated into 50 languages, and millions of copies of the book have been sold.

STORY QUESTIONS

1. Based on reading the passage, what was one of Anne's interests?
   a. playing hopscotch
   b. writing
   c. helping and serving others
   d. playing with her pet dog

2. What can you conclude about Anne Frank?
   a. She was loved and adored by everyone.
   b. She was able to accomplish many things in such a short time period.
   c. She was learning to speak another language.
   d. She lived a courageous life and shared her life in writing.

3. Which of the following statements is not true about Anne Frank?
   a. Anne and her sister, Margot, had to smash batteries.
   b. Anne learned to speak many languages.
   c. On August 4, 1944, the Frank family was betrayed.
   d. She wrote in her diary on a regular basis.

4. What is the main idea of paragraph three?
   a. the descriptions of Anne's first diary entry
   b. Anne's experience of living and working in the concentration camp
   c. the experience of how Anne's family was freed from the camps

LEONARDO DA VINCI

Can you imagine being a famous scientist and a famous painter? It seems like an unusual combination, but that was exactly what Leonardo da Vinci was. He is known as one of the most intelligent people to ever live. He was born and raised in a town in Italy. He learned to paint from a famous artist in the city of Florence.

In the year 1478, he set up his own studio. He became known as the best painter in Florence. Leonardo had a way of painting that made the subjects look like they were real. They had the appearance of moving just as real people moved. Leonardo found the human body interesting, and he would study how it moved and how it worked.

In 1482, he moved to Milan. It was here that he painted one of his most famous paintings. It is called *The Last Supper*. But the paint that he used did not stick to the wall, so he had to repaint it. Leonardo eventually returned to Florence. It was here he painted another very famous painting. This painting is called the *Mona Lisa*. By this time, Leonardo was studying nature. He wanted to learn how birds flew. This interest encouraged him to draw plans for an airplane. He continued studying science after moving to Rome. He also lived in France. He is known throughout the world as a genius.

STORY QUESTIONS

1. Which statement best explains the success of Leonardo da Vinci?
   a. He grew up in a wealthy family.
   b. He learned how to paint from an apprentice.
   c. He was fascinated with life and studied as much as he could.
   d. He was motivated to earn a lot of prize money.

2. Where in the passage does it explain about Leonardo's first famous painting?
   a. first paragraph
   b. end of the second paragraph
   c. second paragraph
   d. beginning of the third paragraph

3. What made Leonardo's paintings with humans so interesting?
   a. He was trying to make them into sculptures and paintings.
   b. The subjects had the appearance of moving like real people.
   c. He was the first to do them in 3-D.
   d. He was the first to do people in oil paintings.

4. What is the author's opinion of Leonardo da Vinci?
   a. unbiased and disinterested
   b. impressed and appreciative
   c. apathetic and interested

ROBERT E. LEE

Robert E. Lee was an American soldier and famous general of the Confederate South. He was born on January 18, 1807. He was the son of a major general and went to West Point in 1825. West Point was a military school. He graduated second in his class. He married Mary Ann Randolph Custis in 1831. They had seven children together. All of his sons would fight in the Civil War.

Lee was a model soldier and was given many awards for his bravery. He became a teacher at West Point. Lee was against slavery and did not want the Southern states to leave the Union. He was asked to be the leader of the U.S., but he turned it down and resigned from the Army. He didn't want to fight against his friends in the South. He was the leader of his state's army in Virginia. Virginia would eventually leave the Union.

On June 1, 1862, Lee became the leader of the Southern army. This army did not have enough uniforms, supplies, or soldiers, but somehow he always managed to win more battles than he lost. But as time went on, Lee was forced to surrender. The Union army was better prepared, and they had a lot more supplies. Lee would spend his last years as a president of a college.

STORY QUESTIONS

1. What is the purpose of the passage?
   a. to inform the reader about the Civil War
   b. to instruct the reader on how to be successful at West Point
   c. to paint a brief picture of the life of Robert E. Lee
   d. to share Lee's interest in the military

2. What is the meaning of the word *resigned* as used in the passage?
   a. talented and exceptional
   b. quit
   c. bestowed with others with a gift
   d. endowed a lot of money

3. What is the main message in this passage about Robert E. Lee?
   a. Know what you want to be early in life so that you don't waste time.
   b. Plan big, for great things might happen.
   c. The more money you make, then the more successful you must be.
   d. Work as hard as you can for those things you believe in.

4. Robert E. Lee is known for . . .
   a. his hard work in impoverished areas.
   b. his interest in U.S. military history.
   c. his great leadership of the Confederate Army.

WOLFGANG AMADEUS MOZART

Mozart is one of the world's most famous composers. You have probably listened to many of the pieces written by Mozart without even knowing it. Mozart's music is so famous that it is used all over world. How did Mozart come to write such beautiful music? Mozart was born in Austria. He was the son of a well-known composer and teacher. Mozart received lessons from his father and was playing before royalty and other important people at the age of six. By the time he was 10 years old, Mozart had traveled all over Europe to play.

It didn't take long for Mozart to begin writing music of his own. He wrote many musical works. Many people could see his talent, but Mozart did not receive pay for writing music. He received money only when he would play. He was forced to give piano lessons to earn enough money to live.

It wasn't until 1780 before Mozart was finally paid to write music. He was given the job to write an opera. He produced his most famous work in the next three years. Mozart was thrilled with his work and opportunity. When Mozart died in 1791, he left a legacy of beautiful music that would impress crowds the world over.

STORY QUESTIONS

1. What is the author's purpose of writing this passage about Mozart?
   a. to share the facts about Mozart
   b. to share the inspiring story of Mozart
   c. to point out that Mozart was not paid enough
   d. to list all works written by Mozart

2. Which sentence from the passage shows how the author feels about Mozart?
   a. He produced his most famous work in the next three years.
   b. How did Mozart come to write such beautiful music?
   c. He received money only when he would play.
   d. By the time he was 10 years old, Mozart had traveled all over Europe to play.

3. Which of the following statements did not happen?
   a. Mozart learned to play beautiful music at a very young age.
   b. Mozart was naturally talented and skilled.
   c. Mozart was paid to play for the president of the United States.
   d. Mozart left a legacy of music that is still played today.

4. Which would be the best title for this passage?
   a. "Mozart vs. the Music World"
   b. "Mozart's Opera"
   c. "Greatest Musicians of all Times"
   d. "The Life of Wolfgang Amadeus Mozart"

THE BATTLE OF ANTIETAM

On September 17, 1862, the bloodiest battle of the Civil War was fought. More lives were lost on this day than on any other day in the history of the country. The North and South were fighting over possession of the Miller Farm cornfield.

General Robert E. Lee was the leader of the Confederate army. He had his men positioned along the banks of the country lane. The general for the Union army was George B. McClellan. This general had a scout that had gotten a copy of the Confederate army's plan. This was very helpful for the Union.

Bullets rained down on the Confederate soldiers. The Union soldiers broke through the line and killed thousands. The country lane where the Confederates were hiding became known as "Bloody Lane" because of all the people who died there.

More than 23,000 men were killed, wounded, or missing in this battle. But the Confederate army was not finished. They would go on to fight another bloody battle with the Union army known as the Battle of Gettysburg.

STORY QUESTIONS

1. Which statement best explains the reason for the Battle of Antietam?
   a. Both sides were fighting over the taxes.
   b. The Confederate soldiers were trying to make a statement.
   c. The Union soldiers were trying to get their independence from Britain.
   d. Both Confederate and Union armies were trying to claim the Miller Farm cornfield.

2. Where in the passage does it explain the advantage that the Union soldiers had at this battle?
   a. first paragraph
   b. second paragraph
   c. third paragraph
   d. fourth paragraph

3. Which of the following statements is false about the Battle of Antietam?
   a. More than 23,000 men were killed, wounded, or missing in this battle.
   b. The North and South were fighting over possession of the Miller Farm cornfield.
   c. More lives were lost on this day than on any other day in the history of the country.
   d. General Lee had a spy that helped him learn his opponent's strategy.

4. What is the author's opinion of the Battle at Antietam?
   a. The author is glad the North won.
   b. The author is impressed and appreciative.
   c. The author has a neutral feeling about it.

THANKSGIVING

Each year, on the fourth Thursday in November, many Americans gather around the table with their families to eat a large feast. Do you know why this is so? It is a celebration of Thanksgiving.

Thanksgiving started back with the Pilgrims. The year was 1621. The Pilgrims had survived a very difficult winter. The next fall they had a great harvest. They were so grateful that they decided to have a feast to celebrate. They invited 91 Native Americans to join them.

The Pilgrims and guests gathered around a large table to eat. There were games, races, and other activities. The celebration lasted three days. We don't know if they really did have turkey, but they did have some kind of bird, as well as venison (meat from deer). They didn't have pumpkin pie because there wasn't enough flour for that. They did have pumpkin that had been boiled and softened. They also had berries, fruit, nuts, and fish.

It wasn't until 1777 that all 13 colonies celebrated Thanksgiving. A lady named Sarah Hale wrote articles in magazines about how important it was to celebrate Thanksgiving. Finally in 1863, President Abraham Lincoln proclaimed Thanksgiving to be celebrated on the fourth Thursday in November. In 1941, Thanksgiving became an official national holiday. Thanksgiving has been celebrated ever since.

STORY QUESTIONS

1. How does the author feel about Thanksgiving?
   a. disgusted
   b. amused
   c. concerned
   d. can't tell from the passage

2. Which statement explains the purpose of Thanksgiving?
   a. Thanksgiving has been celebrated ever since.
   b. They decided to have a feast to celebrate.
   c. Historians have determined that the guests probably gathered around a large table to eat.
   d. They invited 91 Native Americans to join in the feast.

3. The third paragraph informs the reader about . . .
   a. the guests invited to the first Thanksgiving.
   b. how many years it took for Thanksgiving to become official.
   c. the discrimination between the Native Americans and the Pilgrims.
   d. the menu at the first Thanksgiving.

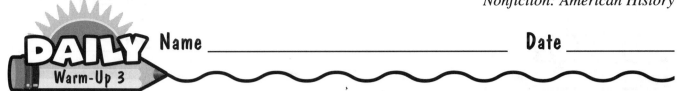

Name _____ Date _____

WAR OF 1812

Some people say that the War of 1812 was the second revolutionary war. In a way, it was. This war was a fight between America and Great Britain. They disagreed about shipping and trade on the seas. Fighting took place in both Canada and America. The Americans won the War of 1812.

Thomas Jefferson was president in America at the time. He was trying to keep American goods going to other parts of the world. He didn't, however, want to get America involved in world events. France and Britain were at war at the time. They both thought that America was supplying the other country with goods and weapons.

Both France and Britain searched American ships. They were treated poorly. America was mad at both countries but ended up fighting Britain. The White House and the Capitol were both burned in the war. A treaty was finally signed. As a result of the war, America became known as a powerful player in the world.

STORY QUESTIONS

1. A good title for this reading passage would be . . .
   a. "Beginnings of the Revolutionary War."
   b. "Britain's Abuse of Power."
   c. "United States Attacked."
   d. "America Caught in the Middle."

2. A similarity between the Revolutionary War and the War of 1812 is . . .
   a. the fact that they were both started with the same U.S. President.
   b. that fighting took place between the U.S. and Great Britain.
   c. that Britain pulled France into the war.
   d. that they took place when the United States was an old country.

3. In the last paragraph, what does the word *player* mean?
   a. performer
   b. actor
   c. interrogator
   d. participant

4. Based on the information in the passage, what caused the War of 1812?
   a. Britain was trying to take over American territory.
   b. France and Britain decided to fight for American territory.
   c. America didn't like how their ships were treated at sea.
   d. France had set up a special arrangement with America.

Name _____   Date _____

A TIME OF REFORM

The early 1900s were a time of reform in the United States. There were many great things about the country, but there were some problems, as well. A group of people who wanted to make changes during this time were called progressives. Many of the city and state governments were corrupt and dishonest. The progressives wanted to change their leaders.

Theodore Roosevelt, who was vice president at the time, was one of the leaders of this reform. He worked with others to change the type of people that were elected to office. They were successful. Led by new leaders, many cities were able to pass new laws that made life better. These cities built schools, parks, and playgrounds. They also built better housing for families.

State governments also worked for change. They passed laws that made large companies pay their fair share of taxes. They put limits on the amount of money they could charge customers for things. With these new changes, the quality of life continued to improve for people.

Theodore Roosevelt eventually became president of the United States upon the assassination of President William McKinley. He continued to work for changes and improvements.

STORY QUESTIONS

1. Based on the passage, what were some of the problems in the country during the early 1900s?
   a. Too many people wanted to be president.
   b. There were not enough jobs for people.
   c. There were dishonest people in leadership positions.
   d. Large companies were not allowed to charge a fair price for goods.

2. What conclusions can be drawn about the people that wanted reform?
   a. They were corrupt and dishonest.
   b. They were hard workers that believed in making changes.
   c. They were inexperienced factory workers.
   d. They weren't very organized.

3. After reading the passage, which of the following statements about the progressives is false?
   a. They were the only ones elected to public office.
   b. They were interested in making life in the United States better.
   c. They were willing to work hard to build schools, parks, and better housing.
   d. They were interested in changing their leaders in city and state office

CHANGES FOR WOMEN

You may be surprised to learn that it took until the 1920s for women in the United States to have the right to vote. Voting wasn't the only change for women during this time. By 1900, women had made a lot of progress. More and more young women were graduating from high school. More young women were also going to college.

In most states, women were beginning to be allowed to own property and keep the money they earned at their jobs. Before then, only the husband could do these things. Anything the wife earned belonged to her husband.

More and more women began working outside of the home. Most of the jobs available were separated into "men's jobs" and "women's jobs." Most women worked as teachers, nurses, librarians, secretaries, factory workers, and telephone operators. Men were the only ones allowed to be doctors, lawyers, bankers, police officers, and mail carriers.

Sweeping changes were still needed. Women continued to fight for the right to work at whatever profession they wanted. Women demanded the same pay that men got. These changes were difficult to make happen. It took many more years. In fact, women today are still working for some of these same things.

STORY QUESTIONS

1. What would be the best title for this reading passage?
    a. "Mr. Mom"
    b. "Sweeping Changes for Women"
    c. "Women's Suffrage"
    d. "The Right to Work"

2. What conclusions can be drawn about what resulted from these changes?
    a. Women were considered illiterate.
    b. Women were given more respect for their abilities.
    c. Men were upset with the changes.
    d. Women were given these rights only if they worked harder.

3. Which statement from the passage explains what limitations women still had after they began working outside the home?
    a. They were inspired to go back to school.
    b. More young women were also going to college.
    c. Women were not allowed to hold the same jobs as men.
    d. Women were not given the right to vote if they worked outside of the home.

MOVING TO THE CITY

Most of the early immigrants came to America to get land and begin farming for a living. But during the late 1800s, it became hard for farmers to make enough money to live. Many of the farmers were forced to give up their farms and move their families to the city in search of jobs. Some farmers left their farms and came to the city to get away from the long hours and loneliness of the farm.

There were different types of jobs available in the city. The city had factories that were being built all over. Women were also able to find jobs in the city.

Living in the city was also exciting. There were many different things to do. The city had museums, theaters, sports, and concert halls. Cities had lots of shopping available. There were stores of all kinds and sizes. Even if you didn't have enough money, window shopping was a favorite pastime. The city had many new opportunities.

The city also had many other resources, such as good schools and teachers. You could also get better medical attention living in the city. Doctors, lawyers, and other professionals were available in the city. More and more people moved to the cities during this time in American history.

STORY QUESTIONS

1. What would be a good title for this reading passage?
   a. "The National Pastime"
   b. "The Lure of the City"
   c. "The Life of a Former Farmer"
   d. "The Big Apple"

2. Which paragraphs explain what the city had to offer?
   a. first and second
   b. third and fourth
   c. second and third
   d. the last three paragraphs

3. Locate the statement below that is <u>not</u> a fact.
   a. There were stores of all kinds and sizes.
   b. Doctors, lawyers, and other professionals were available in the city.
   c. Living in the city was also exciting.
   d. The city had museums, theaters, sports, and concert halls.

4. In this passage, the word *pastime* means . . .
   a. history.
   b. you are late.
   c. a way to spend your time.
   d. long overdue.

BATTLE FOR THE ALAMO

In the 1830s, more and more people from Texas were upset with Mexico. They didn't like the way Mexico was ruling Texas. Texans were beginning to talk about seeking independence from Mexico.

A general from Mexico decided to stop the Texans from making plans to get their independence. His name was Santa Anna. He led an army of 4,000 soldiers to stop the Texans. A group of Texans in San Antonio was attacked. They went to the Alamo for safety. The Alamo was a Spanish mission that had been left empty.

But the Mexican army continued its attack. After 12 days of fighting, the Texans, who were far fewer in number than the Mexicans, ran out of bullets. The Mexican soldiers began climbing the walls. A battle took place inside. Soldiers fought hand to hand. Over 1,500 Mexican soldiers were killed. All but seven of the Texans were killed, and Mexico took back control.

Though they lost, this battle helped the Texans eventually gain their independence and led to the inspirational cry, "Remember the Alamo!"

STORY QUESTIONS

1. What was the purpose for the Texans going to the Alamo?
   a. The Alamo was a Spanish mission that had been left empty.
   b. A group of Texans in San Antonio was attacked.
   c. He led an army of 4,000 soldiers to stop the Texans.
   d. They went to the Alamo for safety.

2. Identify a supporting detail that explains the statement, "A battle took place inside the Alamo."
   a. They went to the Alamo for safety.
   b. The Alamo was a Spanish mission that had been left empty.
   c. Texans were beginning to talk about seeking independence from Mexico.
   d. Over 1,500 Mexican soldiers were killed.

3. After reading the passage, which question couldn't you answer about the Battle for the Alamo?
   a. Who was Santa Anna and for what was he known?
   b. Who were the Texans that were attacked?
   c. What happened after the attack on the Alamo?
   d. How many Mexican soldiers were killed in the Alamo?

Name _____ Date _____

THE QUAKERS

One of the religious groups that immigrated to America was the Quakers. They were also known as the "Society of Friends." The name "Quaker" came from the belief that they thought everyone—even leaders of countries and kings—should "quake" with fear before God.

The Quakers worshipped in a very simple manner. There were no priests or ministers. They believed all people were equal before God. They believed that people should not fight in any wars and they refused to fight in any wars. They believed that all problems could be solved between two countries without any fighting.

The Quakers were not treated very well in England. That was why they left for America. In America, they hoped they would be treated better. Things were not much better in America. They tried to settle in Massachusetts, but they were asked to leave.

William Penn was a Quaker who was able to get land in America from the King of England. This land was named Pennsylvania, which means "Penn's woods." Pennsylvania was set up as a religious experiment. Penn invited religious groups from all over to move to Pennsylvania.

STORY QUESTIONS

1. A good title for this reading passage would be . . .
   a. "The Coming of the Quakers."
   b. "Religion in America."
   c. "Biography of William Penn."
   d. "Pennsylvania Becomes a State."

2. What caused the Quakers to leave England?
   a. The Quakers were forced to leave England.
   b. The Quakers were not allowed to own land in England.
   c. The Quakers were not treated well in England.
   d. The Quakers were not able to convert very many people in England.

3. The author wrote this passage to . . .
   a. justify the Quaker religion.
   b. inform the reader of how Quakers were mistreated in England.
   c. share general information about Massachusetts and the Quakers.
   d. explain the story of the Quakers in America.

Name _____ Date _____

THE WOMEN OF INDEPENDENCE

As the men of America were busy fighting the British over the independence of America, the women of America were busy, too. They wanted to support the American cause in any way that they could. The women did many things that proved to be very helpful.

Many women cared for the wounded soldiers during the battle. They also worked in the army camps washing and cooking. They even made gun powder and would travel to the battlefield to bring water and food to the men. They risked their lives to make the life of the soldiers better. Some women even dressed up to look like men and fought in the war. A large group of women also served as messengers and spies.

Other women helped support the war but never left their homes. They continued to do all of their normal jobs, as well as the work that their husbands and sons would normally do at home. They worked hard to keep the family farms in business. The women felt strongly about their roles during the Revolutionary War. When the story of the Revolutionary War is told, women should always be included in the discussion.

STORY QUESTIONS

1. Based on the reading passage, what interests did women have in the war?
   a. They wanted America to expand and grow.
   b. They were offered a good deal from the army.
   c. They were seeking equal rights for women.
   d. They wanted America to gain independence from England.

2. Which of the following sentences is <u>not</u> something women did to help in the war?
   a. They collected money to send to the troops.
   b. They cared for wounded soldiers.
   c. They kept their family businesses running.
   d. They were spies and messengers.

3. What is the meaning of the word *proved* as used in the first paragraph?
   a. organized
   b. demonstrated
   c. refused
   d. reiterated

4. What is the main idea of paragraph three?
   a. Women helped bring water and food to the soldiers.
   b. Women didn't have to leave home to help fight the war.
   c. The war was not a success without the women.
   d. Women needed to be organized to make a difference.

DAILY Name _____ Date _____
Warm-Up 10

THE IRAN HOSTAGE CRISIS

In 1976, voters elected Jimmy Carter as president of the United States. President Carter worked hard in his presidency to help countries to work together. He was recognized for helping Israel and Egypt agree on a peace treaty.

But things did not go so well in the country of Iran. A revolution had taken place there and the new leader blamed the United States for many of their problems. This leader was very angry with the United States.

A group of rebels from Iran broke into the United States Embassy in Iran and kidnapped 52 hostages. They held these hostages and flashed pictures on the television for the whole world to see. Many demands were made by Iran for the return of the hostages. President Carter refused to make a deal. Iran kept the hostages for more than a year. The United States wasn't able to do anything to gain the release of the hostages.

The hostages were finally released on January 20, 1981. This was the last day of Jimmy Carter's presidency.

STORY QUESTIONS

1. Which of the following statements is inaccurate?
   a. Many demands were made by Iran for the return of the hostages.
   b. President Carter refused to make a deal until the hostages were treated fairly.
   c. The new leader of Iran was very angry with the United States.
   d. Iran kept the hostages for more than a year.

2. Another good title for this reading passage would be . . .
   a. "Crisis Overseas."
   b. "Problems of Foreign Policy."
   c. "Carter vs. Iran."
   d. "Middle East Dilemmas."

3. What is the main idea of the passage?
   a. President Carter was not very effective.
   b. The Iranian leader blamed the U.S. for its problems.
   c. The leader of the Iran was intent on kidnapping more Americans.
   d. Iranian rebels kidnapped 52 hostages during President Carter's term.

4. The hostages were released because . . .
   a. the leader of Iran was definitely afraid of the new president.
   b. the demands were finally met.
   c. the hostages were able to be released through talks.
   d. This question cannot be answered based on the passage.

THE SLAVE TRADE

In the late 1600s, the cost of buying a slave went down. The colonies in America began buying more and more slaves. These slaves came from the continent of Africa. People in Africa were captured and sold as slaves throughout the world.

Slave traders hunted for young men and women and captured them in nets and traps. They were taken from their families and villages. They would never return home again. Thousands and thousands of people were captured and sold as slaves. The new slave owners branded them like cattle so people would know to whom the slaves belonged. They were treated terribly.

The slaves were packed onto ships and sent across the ocean. Many of the slaves were sold and sent to the West Indies. They worked on sugar farms there. Some of the slaves were also sent to America at this time. People in the southern colonies bought many of the slaves to work on the large plantations. They worked in the tobacco, cotton, and rice fields. The life of a slave was terrible and inhumane.

STORY QUESTIONS

1. How does the author feel about how the captured slaves were treated?
   a. tolerant
   b. confused
   c. disgusted
   d. accepting

2. Which of the following sentences portrays the author's opinion about the captured slaves?
   a. The cost of slaves had gone down.
   b. Thousands and thousands of these people were captured and sold as slaves.
   c. Many of the slaves were sold and sent to the West Indies.
   d. The life of a slave was terrible and inhumane.

3. Which of the following statements is one of the reasons slaves were sold to the southern plantations?
   a. Plantation owners could afford slaves and needed the workers.
   b. Plantation owners worked together to grow crops.
   c. The weather was good so that crops could be grown year-round, which meant that they needed more workers.
   d. The plantation owners wanted to brand their slaves.

4. What is meant by the word *hunted* as used in this passage?
   a. sought after
   b. organizing
   c. refused
   d. treated like captive animals

DAILY Warm-Up 12

Name _____ Date _____

A PRESIDENT RESIGNS

Richard Nixon was elected president of the United States in 1968 and took office in 1969. His first term was spent in building better relationships with China and the Soviet Union. When his first term as president ended, he had made a lot of progress.

In 1972, Nixon ran for a second term as president. He was running for the Republican Party. Four men who were working on his reelection team broke into the Democratic Party headquarters. This was illegal. The headquarters were in the Watergate Hotel. The break-in became known as the Watergate scandal. The men that broke in were looking for information they could use against Nixon's opponent in the campaign.

The men were caught. At first, President Nixon denied any connection with these men. He lied about knowing about the break-in. It took two years for the truth to come out. Nixon had lied about knowing about the break-in and his connection with the men.

Congress could vote to remove Nixon from office. Nixon decided to resign. He was the first president ever to resign. When President Nixon resigned, Gerald Ford was vice president. Ford became the new president of the United States.

STORY QUESTIONS

1. Which paragraph explains when Nixon finally resigned?
   a. first paragraph
   b. last paragraph
   c. third paragraph
   d. second paragraph

2. After reading the passage, what inference can you make about why Nixon resigned?
   a. He didn't want to be kicked out of office by Congress.
   b. He knew there would be more investigations.
   c. His lawyer counseled him to resign.
   d. The American people demanded that he resign.

3. What is the author's opinion about the Nixon resignation?
   a. The author thinks that it was a great day when Nixon resigned.
   b. The author thinks there has not been enough research on why Nixon resigned.
   c. The author is interested in sharing the process of how a president resigns from office.
   d. The author is trying to inform the reader about President Nixon's resignation.

Name _____ Date _____

THE KOREAN WAR

Korea is a country in Asia. Japan began ruling Korea in the early 1900s. By the end of World War II, Japan had lost control of Korea. The Soviet Union was given control of North Korea. The United States was given control of South Korea. As time went on, the two halves of Korea became enemies of each other.

In 1950, North Korea attacked South Korea. The United Nations knew that it had to help South Korea. It sent troops and supplies to help South Korea. Most of the troops, supplies, and weapons came from the United States.

The United Nations armies were able to push back the North Korean troops. It looked like the South Koreans had been able to defeat the North Koreans. But then China got involved. They sent a large army to help the North Koreans. They used their army to drive back the U.N. army.

Finally, in 1953, the two sides of the armies agreed to stop fighting. The boundary between the two Korean sides was set up again. To this day, North and South Korea are still two different countries.

STORY QUESTIONS

1. How did the Korean War get its name?
   a. The war took place in Asia.
   b. The war was given its name after the country of Korea came together as one.
   c. The war got its name after China came to rescue North Korea.
   d. The war took place between the North and South Korean countries.

2. What is the purpose of the third paragraph?
   a. to explain why the Soviet Union got involved
   b. to explain the shift in the Korean War
   c. to explain how the U.S became involved in the war
   d. to explain how Korean was divided up

3. Which paragraph would you read to find out about who controlled Korea at the beginning of the 20th century?
   a. first paragraph
   b. third paragraph
   c. second paragraph
   d. fourth paragraph

THE LUSITANIA

During World War I, the Germans were using underwater boats, or submarines, to attack the enemy at sea. These submarines were called U-boats, which stood for "undersea boats." They could sink large ships by firing torpedoes underneath the water. The Germans gave no warning and could kill everyone on board. The German navy was making great strides at sea.

The Germans decided to start attacking passenger ships, as well as cargo ships. On May 7, 1915, a German U-boat shot and sank a British passenger ship. The name of the ship was the *Lusitania*. This ship was shot off the coast of Ireland and sank.

The attack killed over 1,200 people. Both adults and children were killed in this attack. Of those who were killed, 128 were Americans. This made the American public very angry.

President Wilson insisted that Germans had to give warning before shooting torpedoes at ships. This worked for a while, until the Germans decided they didn't want to do this anymore. After the Germans attacked three American ships, the United States became involved in World War I. In April 1917, the U.S. declared war on Germany.

STORY QUESTIONS

1. Which of the following statements can be inferred after reading the passage?
   a. The *Lusitania* was a turning point for the United States getting involved in World War I.
   b. People were interested in the U.S. building a U-boat.
   c. The Germans were seeking revenge on the United States.
   d. There were no children on the *Lusitania*.

2. The purpose of the first paragraph is to . . .
   a. introduce the reason why the U.S. got involved in World War I.
   b. explain the differences between the German and American armies.
   c. compare the reasons for World War I.
   d. give background of what was going on at sea during World War I.

3. Pick the word that best completes the sentence, "The Germans decided not to listen to the _____ from the U.S. about attacking ships at sea."
   a. advice
   b. demands
   c. warning
   d. acknowledgement

THE RISE OF THE COMMON MAN

On March 4, 1829, twenty thousand Americans came to Washington, D.C. They wanted to watch Andrew Jackson be sworn in as president. Jackson was very popular. He was especially popular with the "common" people of the United States. The large crowd ended up breaking dishes and getting out of control at the White House. President Jackson had to spend his first night at a hotel.

All of this was a result of big changes that were happening in America. Before this time, only adult white males were allowed to vote. But not just any adult white male could vote: he had to own property and pay taxes.

The changes that happened in the late 1820s were that any adult white male—whether or not they owned property or paid taxes—could vote. This was called the "rise of the common man."

Women, blacks, and Native Americans were still not allowed to vote, but giving all adult white males the right to vote was a big step in the right direction. The spirit of democracy and equality was higher than ever before.

STORY QUESTIONS

1. Why were so many people at the swearing in of Andrew Jackson as president?
   a. the treatment of the common man
   b. the lack of civil rights for all citizens of America
   c. the participation of more people in the election
   d. the misunderstanding of the government

2. Which paragraph would help you answer the previous question?
   a. second paragraph.
   b. first paragraph
   c. fourth paragraph
   d. third paragraph

3. Which of the following statements is <u>not</u> true about Andrew Jackson?
   a. He was president during the rise of the "common man."
   b. He fought for civil rights of all men and women.
   c. He was a popular candidate.
   d. He spent his first night as president in a hotel.

4. What is the meaning of the word *common* as used in this passage?
   a. peculiar
   b. abnormal
   c. everyday
   d. estranged

THE PANAMA CANAL

In the early 1900s, the United States decided that they wanted to build a canal that would connect the Atlantic and Pacific Oceans. Ships would not have to travel as far. This would make the travel and trade between the oceans much faster.

France had tried to do the same thing 20 years earlier. They weren't able to do it. In 1903, the land of Panama belonged to the country of Colombia. President Theodore Roosevelt tried to pay Colombia for the strip of land so that they could build the canal. The government of Colombia didn't think it was enough money for the land.

President Roosevelt was upset. He knew there was a group of rebels from Panama that wanted to separate from Colombia. President Roosevelt decided to help them. He sent ships that prevented the Colombian army from landing in Panama. Panama won without a fight. Panama sold the strip of land to the United States.

Building the canal was a lot of work. Jungles had to be cleared and a lot of land had to be moved. Workers also had to fight the mosquitoes. The mosquitoes transmitted terrible diseases. Finally, an army doctor got rid of the mosquitoes by not allowing them to breed. The first ship sailed through the Panama Canal in August of 1914.

STORY QUESTIONS

1. How did Roosevelt get the land for the Panama Canal?
   a. He ordered a change of government in Panama.
   b. He ignored the Colombian government and built the canal anyway.
   c. He got the votes needed to make the change.
   d. He supported the independence of Panama.

2. Which paragraph helps you answer the previous question?
   a. second paragraph
   b. first paragraph
   c. fourth paragraph
   d. third paragraph

3. Which of the following statements is <u>not</u> true about building of the Panama Canal?
   a. It was finally opened in August of 1914.
   b. The mosquitoes were a big problem when building the canal.
   c. The jungles were able to be preserved when the canal was built.
   d. It was a lot of work to move the land for the canal.

SATURN

Saturn is the sixth planet from our sun. This amazing planet is best known for its rings. We may think that these rings are small in number, but when seen through a telescope, there are hundreds of them. The rings of Saturn are made up of very tiny pieces of matter. There are so many objects floating that from a distance, they look like solid rings. The rings are also very thin. The rings are made up of rocky ice particles and dust. Saturn also has many moons.

Galileo was the first person to look at Saturn through a telescope. The year was 1610. He was amazed at what he could see, but he didn't understand it. The telescopes today are much better and can reveal the intricate details of the rings and moons.

Another interesting fact about Saturn is that it could float. That seems surprising because Saturn is the second-largest planet. Even though it is big, it doesn't weigh very much. It is less dense less than water. Saturn rotates very quickly, which means that a day on Saturn is only about 10 hours long. Saturn is made up mostly of hydrogen and helium. There have been many unmanned trips to get a closer look at Saturn. Four spacecrafts have taken pictures and visited Saturn. These were the *Pioneer 11, Voyager 1, Voyager 2,* and *Cassini.*

STORY QUESTIONS

1. What would be the best title for this passage?
   a. "Saturn: The Planet with Rings"
   b. "Outer Planets"
   c. "Low-Density Planets"
   d. "Planets with Moons"

2. According to the passage, which of the following is not a fact about the planet Saturn?
   a. Saturn is the second-largest planet.
   b. A day on Saturn is about 10 hours long.
   c. Saturn has a great red spot.
   d. Saturn rotates very quickly.

3. What is one reason why humans cannot live on Saturn?
   a. Saturn has more rings than other planets.
   b. Saturn is so light it could float.
   c. Saturn rotates quicker than Earth.
   d. Saturn is made up of mostly hydrogen and helium.

4. How did the telescope change what people thought about Saturn?
   a. Saturn was the first planet viewed through a telescope.
   b. Galileo discovered that Saturn had rings.
   c. It was determined that Saturn was not located in a star's position.
   d. Saturn was discovered to be the center of the universe.

GEOLOGY

Geology is the study of the history of Earth. It is thought that Earth is about 4.6 billion years old. It has a very long history. Rocks provide a lot of important information about what happened in the past. Geologists study rocks to determine how they were made.

There are a few rocks that are made of just one mineral—such as marble or quartzite—but most rocks are made up of more than one mineral. Most rocks have elements such as silicon, carbon, iron, and oxygen.

The outer layer of the Earth is called the crust. At this point, we are not able to directly study anything below the Earth's crust. We are only able to drill down a few miles. This makes it difficult to study what is going on inside the Earth, but rocks and the ground are constantly being shuffled and pushed around through the years.

One way that rocks are formed and built up is from volcanic activity. Magma lies beneath the Earth's crust and is forced to the surface. Rocks are moved and overturned from earthquakes. All rocks are broken down by a process called weathering. The weather plays a role in erosion and the breakdown of rocks. Water, rain, ice, and wind all contribute to the breaking down of rocks.

STORY QUESTIONS

1. Which statement explains how scientists learn about the history of the Earth?
    a. All rocks break down by being exposed to the weather.
    b. Geologists study rocks to determine how they were made.
    c. All rocks are combinations of one or more minerals.
    d. One way that rocks are formed and built up is from volcanic activity.

2. The main idea of this passage is . . .
    a. to inform the reader about what happens when a volcano explodes.
    b. to inform the reader about the connection between the earth's crust and rocks.
    c. to inform the reader about how important erosion is to breaking down rocks.
    d. to share general information about the geology and the study of rocks.

3. Where can you find information about how rocks are formed and broken down?
    a. second paragraph
    b. not in the passage
    c. fourth paragraph
    d. third paragraph

STATIC ELECTRICITY

Have you ever seen your hair sticking straight up in the air all by itself? Or how about the last time you dragged your foot across the floor and got a shock? This was probably static electricity. But how does static electricity work?

Everything is made up of atoms. Particles called electrons are part of every atom. These electrons have an electric charge. This charge is negative and is the cause of electricity.

Static electricity isn't really static at all. It involves electrons that move from one place to another. Static electricity is different because it doesn't flow from one place to another in a current like most electricity.

Electrons move from one object to another by vigorous rubbing or brushing. There is an electric field around each object. The field affects objects and produces unlike charges in them. The unlike charges are attracted to each other. Sometimes static electricity makes a popping sound.

STORY QUESTIONS

1. Which of the following statements is true but not found in the reading passage?
   a. This charge is negative and is the cause of electricity.
   b. Static electricity is more common in the dry, winter air.
   c. Sometimes static electricity makes a popping sound.
   d. Static electricity gets its name because it involves electrons that move from one place to another.

2. Which of the following statements can you infer after reading the passage?
   a. Static electricity does not last long, but ends quickly.
   b. Static electricity is very dangerous.
   c. Scientists still do not know how static electricity works.
   d. Static electricity only happens to certain people.

3. There is an electric _____ around each object.
   a. charge
   b. span
   c. shortage
   d. field

4. The purpose of the third paragraph is to . . .
   a. inform the reader about how static electricity begins.
   b. inform the reader about how static electricity works.
   c. inform the reader on how best to prevent static electricity.

VOLCANOES

What is a volcano? Volcanoes are mountains, but they aren't typical mountains. Volcanoes are formed when magma (hot, liquid rock) rises up from beneath and leaks into the Earth's crust, or surface level. It forms a pool beneath the surface called a magma chamber. As this pool gets bigger, it swells the earth on top of it upwards and outwards.

The term *volcano* comes from Vulcan, the Roman god of fire and metalworking. It was originally believed that smoke and fire from volcanoes was evidence that Vulcan was doing his metalwork inside of them. A small island was named Vulcano because of its many volcanoes.

Volcanoes erupt when the pressure of the magma beneath the surface becomes too great for the rock above it to contain. At this point, the magma breaks through the surface—sometimes in a great explosion—at which point it is called lava.

The temperature inside a volcano is very hot. Scientists say it can get as hot as 2,120 degrees Fahrenheit. Molten rock turns an orange-yellow color when it reaches 900 degrees. When it cools to 630 degrees, the color becomes dark to bright cherry red.

STORY QUESTIONS

1. What does the word *evidence* mean as used in the passage?
   a. argument
   b. proof
   c. instruction
   d. plan

2. What does a volcanic eruption depend on?
   a. It depends on the amount of air pressure around the volcano.
   b. It depends on the amount of past action from the volcano.
   c. It depends on the pressure of the magma against the surface above it.
   d. It depends on how many years it has been since it last erupted.

3. Which paragraph helps answer the previous question?
   a. first paragraph
   b. fourth paragraph
   c. second paragraph
   d. third paragraph

4. Which of the following statements is a fact about volcanoes?
   a. Volcanoes are made from erosion.
   b. Volcanoes are mountains.
   c. Volcanoes have a vent which is connected to molten rock.
   d. The temperature inside a volcano is warm.

Name _____ Date _____

THE RAIN FOREST

One of the most talked about places in the world is the rain forest. This amazing ecosystem has more species and plants than all the other ecosystems in the world combined. There are more than 10 million species. Scientists say that there are even species that haven't been identified yet.

The rain forest is a lush and green place. It is called the rain forest because it rains a lot. It may begin raining at a moment's notice. Constant thunderstorms lead to a lot of flooding and very wet soil. It is also a very hot and humid place. The climate remains the same all the time. This consistency in climate creates a stable environment for many plants and animals. The largest rain forests can be found in the African Congo, the Amazon Basin in South America, and Southern Asia.

There is a lot of concern about the amount of rain forest that is being destroyed. Animals and plant species become extinct when their environment is destroyed. Scientists say that over 500 square miles of the rain forest is destroyed every minute. That's a lot of destruction!

Why is the rain forest being destroyed? There are many different reasons. One of the reasons is so that farmers can make fields to grow plants. The rain forest is also chopped down to use the wood for things like furniture. Organizations have been set up to try and keep people from cutting down any more rain forests.

STORY QUESTIONS

1. Which of the following statements is contained in the passage about the rain forest?
   a. Scientists use the rain forest to study plant and animal species.
   b. The rain forest has been around for millions of years.
   c. Money has been raised to save the rain forest.
   d. The climate of the rain forest remains constant.

2. Which paragraph helps you answer the previous question?
   a. second paragraph
   b. first paragraph
   c. fourth paragraph
   d. third paragraph

3. Without the rain, what would probably happen to the rain forest?
   a. It could not withstand the sun's ultraviolet rays.
   b. There would be no weather patterns.
   c. There would be more destruction of the rain forest.
   d. It would dry up and some plants and animals could not survive.

THE POLAR REGIONS

The polar regions are the coldest places on the Earth. The temperatures there have gotten as low as –126 degrees Fahrenheit. The sea is covered with a thick layer of ice. Days are very long in the polar regions. The sun doesn't set during three to four of the summer months. Though there is a lot of sun, it doesn't provide very much warmth. It doesn't rain very often, either, but there is snow on the ground.

The living conditions in the polar regions are extreme. Plants cannot grow, but there are some animals that are able to survive. Some of these animals are the seal, walrus, polar bear, wolf, caribou, whale, and the arctic fox. These animals have adapted to this climate. For example, the polar bear has a thick layer of fat under its fur coat. This helps keep it warm.

Along the outer edges of the polar region and the ice caps, the ground is frozen solid. In the warmer months, mosses and other plants can grow there. Reindeer live along the edges and eat some of the plants that grow on the outer edges. People who once lived in these frozen climates used reindeer. Today, most of these people live in cities and towns instead of on the frozen countryside.

STORY QUESTIONS

1. How are reindeer able to live along the outer edges of the ice caps?
   a. The snow has melted off the ice caps.
   b. The reindeer eat the moss and other plants that grow past the ice caps.
   c. The people from long ago brought the reindeer to this region.
   d. The reindeer feed on the animals that live in the polar regions.

2. What is the purpose of the second paragraph?
   a. to explain how the polar regions were developed
   b. to explain how the animals in this area survive
   c. to explain how people in the past lived in the polar regions
   d. to explain where the plants grow in the polar regions

3. Where in the passage would you read to find out about the temperatures in the polar regions?
   a. first paragraph
   b. end of the third paragraph
   c. second paragraph
   d. end of the second paragraph

4. What is the meaning of the word *adapted* as used in this passage?
   a. arranged
   b. distinct
   c. modified
   d. opposite

THE TELESCOPE

Since the beginning of time, man has been trying to look beyond what the human eye can see. Hans Lippershey, a man from the Netherlands, invented the telescope in 1608. The Dutch government tried to keep the invention a secret, but it didn't work out that way. Galileo heard about it and built his own, more powerful telescope in 1609. A telescope uses a magnifying lens to focus light coming from things at a great distance. Today, astronomers still use telescopes to look at distant stars, planets, and other wonders in space.

There are two main types of telescopes. The first type is called the refracting telescope. This telescope helps you see things at a relatively short distance. This type of telescope is used at tourist sights to help you see scenic views. They were also used in the past by sea captains to help them find their way at sea. A refracting telescope has two lenses at either end of the tube. The largest lens is at the far end of the telescope. Light shines through to the smaller lens, which is called the eyepiece. The image is magnified. The image in a simple refracting telescope is upside down.

The other type of telescope is the reflecting telescope. Reflecting telescopes use mirrors instead of lenses. The mirrors focus the light onto the eyepiece. The reflecting telescope is much more expensive. Some of the bigger reflecting telescopes are made using large mirrors. Oftentimes, they are set high up on mountains so that they will be above the clouds and can give people a clear view.

STORY QUESTIONS

1. What does the word *relatively* mean as used in the passage?
   a. extraordinary
   b. rather
   c. inhibited
   d. progressive

2. What is the main idea of this reading passage?
   a. to inform the reader about the early telescopes that were used in ancient times
   b. to inform the reader about how a telescope is operated
   c. to explain the difference between the two different types of telescopes
   d. to explain the life of Galileo and his inventions

3. Which of the following statements is <u>not</u> true regarding refracting and reflecting telescopes?
   a. The reflecting telescope is used to see things far away.
   b. The refracting telescope shows the image upside down.
   c. The refracting telescope uses lenses while a reflecting telescope uses mirrors.
   d. Galileo invented the telescope.

Name _____ Date _____

WAVES

How many times have you sat on a beach and looked at the ocean? It is an amazing sight. The waves are fun to splash in, but have you ever wondered what causes waves and how they work? Waves can be gentle and lapping, or they can be rolling and crash onto the shore. What makes the difference?

When you are sitting on the beach, it looks like the waves are rushing right at you. But that is really not the case. The water in a wave is actually rising up out of the water and then coming back down. It usually comes back down in the same or very similar position.

Out at sea, a wave can travel a great distance. Waves can move large ships and other large objects. But once a wave gets closer to the shore, it does not have as much power. It begins to slow down and drag. The top part of the wave keeps going. When you see the cap on a wave, it means that the wave is "breaking" before it goes down under water again.

The wind is usually what causes surface waves. The wind can be blowing hard or it can be blowing softly. The more intense the wind is, the higher the wave will be. The wind pushes the water.

STORY QUESTIONS

1. Which paragraph does not explain how waves work?
   a. first paragraph
   b. second paragraph
   c. third paragraph
   d. fourth paragraph

2. What is the author's opinion about the ocean?
   a. The author thinks the ocean needs to be cleaned up.
   b. The author thinks there has not been enough research about how waves work.
   c. The author is interested in sharing the wonders of animal life in the ocean.
   d. The author thinks the ocean and the waves are amazing.

3. Which sentence expresses the author's feelings about the ocean?
   a. Out at sea, a wave can travel a great distance.
   b. Waves can move large ships and other large objects.
   c. It is an amazing sight.
   d. The more intense the wind is, the higher the wave will be.

Name _____

Date _____

FOSSILS

Have you ever seen a fossil in rocks buried in the earth? It's like finding a treasure. Fossils are remains of plants and animals that lived a very long time ago. For example, any dinosaur fossil that is found is at least 65 million years old.

Fossils tell stories about the past. Many of these stories are surprising. For example, fossils of sea life have been found as high up as the top of Mount Everest. This means that at one point, the rocks in Mt. Everest were probably under water. Fossils from plants in the rain forest have been buried deep in the ice of the South Pole.

The oldest known fossil is a tiny bacterium. These fossils have been found in Southern Africa. These fossils are said to be as old as 3.5 billion years.

How are fossils formed? Bones and plant remains begin to decay with time. But sometimes, the bones and plant remains are covered with mud or sand. This makes it possible for the soft parts to decay, while the harder parts (such as wood, bones, and teeth) last a lot longer. Eventually, these hard parts become hardened or petrified.

STORY QUESTIONS

1. What is the meaning of the word *petrified* as used in the passage?
   a. scared
   b. stiff
   c. excitable
   d. rotten

2. What is the purpose of the third paragraph?
   a. to explain how fossils are formed
   b. to mention the oldest fossil found
   c. to explain how fossils are found
   d. to explain what happens to fossils after they are found

3. Which paragraph would you read to find out about unusual places that fossils have been found?
   a. first paragraph
   b. third paragraph
   c. fourth paragraph
   d. second paragraph

4. Which sentence explains how fossils begin to be formed?
   a. Fossils tell stories about the past.
   b. Fossils are remains of plants and animals that lived a very long time ago.
   c. But sometimes, the bones and plant remains are covered with mud or sand.
   d. Fossils from plants in the rain forest have been buried deep in the ice of the South Pole.

LATITUDE AND LONGITUDE

The Earth is a very large surface, and at times it is very hard to explain exactly where you are. There are two types of directions that can be used. The first type is absolute direction. Absolute direction is when you are given a specific address of a location, such as a street address. The other type of direction is relative. Relative direction uses imaginary lines called latitude and longitude lines to explain location. These imaginary lines run from north to south and east to west across the Earth.

Latitude lines run east to west. These lines are used to tell you how far north or south you are from the equator. The equator is the imaginary line that runs horizontally along the center of the Earth. It is the exact midpoint between the North and South Poles.

Latitude lines are also called parallels because they go around the Earth without ever crossing or intersecting. They are numbered from 0 to 90 degrees. Zero degrees is found at the equator. The North Pole is 90 degrees north and the South Pole is 90 degrees south.

There are other imaginary lines that run north to south. These imaginary lines are called longitudinal lines. The very center line that runs through the North and South poles is called the prime meridian. The prime meridian divides the globe into two half circles called the Eastern and Western hemispheres. Lines of longitude are also called meridian lines. Lines of latitude and longitude can help you find your location and place on this earth.

STORY QUESTIONS

1. What would be the best title for this passage?
   a. "Parallel Lines"
   b. "Imaginary Lines of Direction"
   c. "How Latitude Lines Work"
   d. "Eastern and Western Hemisphere"

2. Which of the following is <u>not</u> a fact about latitude lines?
   a. Latitude lines are also called parallels.
   b. Latitude lines run east to west.
   c. Latitude lines divide the Earth into two hemispheres.
   d. Latitude lines run north and south of the equator.

3. Lines of latitude and longitude help you determine which type of direction?
   a. relative
   b. absolute
   c. direct
   d. none of the above

DESERT LIFE

Living in the desert usually means extreme heat and dry, arid conditions. There are different types of deserts. Some deserts have more plant life than other deserts. The largest desert in the world is the Sahara Desert. This desert covers over a million square miles of land.

Like all deserts, the Sahara has very little vegetation. However, there are some plants that have learned to grow without very much rain. Cacti are examples of plants that can live for almost a year without rain. When a cactus does receive rain, it produces beautiful and striking flowers.

Many of the animals that live in the desert are the same color as the environment. These sand-colored animals often burrow into the sand to avoid the extreme heat. Many of these animals are nocturnal animals, which means they feed and are active mostly during the night. When there is a severe drought, many of these animals sleep to save water and their need for food.

Camels are another type of animal commonly found in the Sahara Desert. The camel is able to go for a week without any drinking water. The camel's hump serves as food storage. A camel will drink up to 16 gallons of water at one time.

STORY QUESTIONS

1. Why are desert animals nocturnal?
   a. The sun is too bright during the day.
   b. They are trying to avoid the extreme heat.
   c. The water comes at night.
   d. They are able to move faster.

2. According to the passage, why are camels good animals for working in the desert?
   a. There is no specific reason listed.
   b. They work together to help each other in extremely hot conditions.
   c. They are able to store food and water and go without water for a long time.
   d. They have always been used in the desert.

3. What is the main idea of the passage?
   a. to show how camels store food and water
   b. to list the types of animals found in the desert
   c. to explain what plant life and animal life is like in the desert
   d. to show how cacti can survive a drought

4. What do animals that live in the desert have in common?
   a. They are all reptiles.
   b. They are all nocturnal animals.
   c. They have learned to adapt to the heat.
   d. They are brightly-colored animals.

DAILY
Warm-Up 12

Name _____ Date _____

PLUTO

Pluto used to be considered the planet farthest from the sun in our solar system. A scientist named Clyde W. Tombaugh accidentally discovered Pluto in 1930. At the time, Clyde was working at the Lowell Observatory in Flagstaff, Arizona and discovered Pluto after doing a very thorough search of the night sky. Pluto's moon, Charon, was discovered in 1978. Pluto orbits a star, our sun, every 248 years. It is a round body that is about 1,429 miles (2300 km) wide. There has been controversy over Pluto ever since it was discovered. Many wanted it classified as a comet or asteroid rather than a planet. Pluto was always considered a planet until a vote by astronomers on August 24, 2006 reclassified it as a dwarf planet.

The International Astronomical Union (IAU) defined a planet as "an object that orbits the sun and is large enough to have become round due to the force of its own gravity." It also stated that the object has to have cleared its orbit of other objects, namely, that it is larger than its surrounding objects. Charon, Pluto's one moon, is about half its size, whereas the moons of the traditional planets are much smaller than their planets. Therefore, Pluto does not "dominate" its area of space. It also has an unusual orbit that overlaps the orbit of Neptune, making it closer to Earth than Neptune for 20 years out of its 248-year orbit.

Many astronomers disagree with the new classification of Pluto. Although Pluto is much smaller than any of the other planets in our solar system, it is more like Earth than Jupiter or Saturn. Pluto and Earth have solid surfaces, while Jupiter and Saturn are made of gas. Some astronomers also bring up the point that less than 5% of astronomers worldwide voted on the new definition of a planet that demoted Pluto to a dwarf planet. There are already petitions being made to reinstate Pluto to its previous status. What do you think? Is Pluto a planet?

STORY QUESTIONS

1. Pluto was reclassified as a dwarf planet after a vote by . . .
   a. less than 25% of astronomers
   b. less than 15% of astronomers
   c. less than 35% of astronomers
   d. less than 5% of astronomers

2. Other words that can be used in place of *accidentally* are . . .
   a. by protection.
   b. by mistake.
   c. by structure.
   d. by formation.

3. If you wanted to study about the orbit of Pluto, would this passage be helpful?
   a. Yes, it is very helpful.
   b. No, there is not enough information.
   c. Yes, it provides a little information on that topic.
   d. No, it is not reliable information.

4. Pluto has one moon named . . .
   a. Neptune.
   b. Io.
   c. Charon.
   d. Charlie.

ON THE MOUNTAIN TOP

It is an exhilarating feeling to stand at the top of a mountain and look down. There are amazing views. You can tell by looking at a mountain which plants can grow at different heights. The higher you go up the mountain, the colder it is. For every 820 feet you climb, the temperature drops one degree. If you look at the very top of a high mountain, there is usually no or very little vegetation or plants there. Icy wind blows and prevents trees from growing. When mountains get higher than 8,200 feet, there is a timberline. Trees cannot grow above the timberline.

The trees along the mountainside help to protect the mountain soil. This prevents the mountain soil from eroding. When there is too much erosion, there are problems with flooding and landslides. In the wintertime, these cleared-off areas can trigger avalanches.

It is very common to see conifer trees growing on mountains. Most conifers are called evergreens, which means they stay green all of the time. They do not lose their leaves like other trees. The leaves on evergreens are needles. When old needles fall off, they are replaced with new ones. Conifers are able to handle the harsh weather conditions of the mountains. They can survive the cold and the elements.

There are also other types of trees that grow on mountains. In lower portions of the mountain, you can find chestnut, oak, and maple trees.

STORY QUESTIONS

1. What is this passage mainly about?
   a. how tall mountains can get
   b. how trees grow below the timberline
   c. how conifer trees lose their needles and then replace them
   d. the different types of trees that can grow on mountains

2. Why does the temperature get cooler the higher you go up the mountain?
   a. The temperature drops as air pressure rises.
   b. The temperature drops because there are no trees.
   c. The temperature drops because of the higher elevation.
   d. The temperature drops because conifer trees can't grow above the timberline.

3. According to the passage, what are the two main factors that create harsh conditions?
   a. snow and hail
   b. sleet and snow
   c. wind and cold temperatures
   d. cold temperatures and hail

ACIDS AND BASES

Have you ever heard the terms *acid* and *base*? Acids and bases play important roles in your life. Acids and bases can be found in just about everything. Almost every liquid you see is either an acid or a base. The only liquid that is not an acid or a base is distilled water.

An acid has more hydrogen ions. The word *acid* comes from the Latin word *acidus*, which means "sharp." Acids usually have a sour taste. Examples of acids are lemon juice and vinegar. Most citrus fruits have a lot of acids, as do teas and yogurt. Not all acids can be eaten. Some of them can be very harmful. Some acids can burn holes in clothing or skin. These strong acids are used to produce dyes, plastic, fertilizers, and more.

A base is a bitter-tasting chemical. Egg whites and ammonia are bases. Soap is also made from a base. Did you know that your blood is a base? There are many bases that can be eaten, but there are many that are very dangerous to touch, taste, or smell.

Acids and bases are opposites. So when you mix them together, they can neutralize each other. Mixing them together takes a bit of potency away and makes them weaker. When there is too much of an acid, a base will be added to counteract the acidity. Gardeners are constantly working to get the right balance in the soil. If there is too much acid, plants won't grow.

STORY QUESTIONS

1. Which of the following statements is true?
   a. Acids and bases are both dangerous to your body.
   b. Bases are the weakened form of acids.
   c. Acids and bases should never be mixed together.
   d. Acids and bases can be found in just about everything.

2. Which sentence from the passage supports the previous statement?
   a. The only liquid that is not an acid or a base is distilled water.
   b. Almost every liquid you see is either an acid or a base.
   c. Most citrus fruits have a lot of acids, as do teas and yogurt.
   d. These strong acids are used to produce dyes, plastic, fertilizers, and more.

3. Which question could be answered after reading this passage?
   a. What are some examples of acids and bases?
   b. Does a banana have acids in it?
   c. How do I neutralize the acids and bases in the food I eat?
   d. What is the pH scale?

4. What is the meaning of word *potency* in this passage?
   a. influence
   b. strength
   c. speed
   d. understood

CRICKET TEMPERATURE

Have you ever listened to the chirping of the crickets on a summer evening? Did you know that the cricket's chirp can help you determine the temperature outside?

Crickets are black or brownish insects. They are cold-blooded, which means their body temperature is the same as the temperature of their surroundings. If the temperature outside is warm, then the cricket's body temperature is warm.

During the hot summer months, the crickets are more active. You can hear them chirping or "singing." This noise is made when the cricket rubs the bases of its back legs together. The hotter it is, the faster the cricket will rub its legs together.

You can figure out the temperature outside by following a simple formula using the chirps of the cricket. First, you count the number of cricket chirps per minute. You divide that number by the number four. Then you add that number to 40. Surprisingly enough, the answer you get is pretty close to the actual temperature outside. It is usually only one or two degrees off. Try it sometime!

STORY QUESTIONS

1. Why does the author say, "Surprisingly enough, the answer you get is pretty close to the actual temperature outside"?
   a. Because it seems too easy to figure out the temperature that way.
   b. Because it seems to be a very precise formula.
   c. Because it doesn't seem like it would be a very accurate way to determine the temperature.
   d. Because it does not seem very probable that the cricket chirp will be predictable.

2. What is the main idea of the second paragraph?
   a. to explain the cricket and how its body adjusts to temperature
   b. to explain how the cricket makes the chirping noise
   c. to explain how to determine the temperature using the cricket chirps
   d. to explain why the cricket chirps only in the summer months

3. What is the meaning of the term "singing" in the third paragraph?
   a. smaller or lesser
   b. disconcerting
   c. bothering
   d. tweeting

4. Crickets are more active in the . . .
   a. outdoors.
   b. kitchen.
   c. cooler months.
   d. warmer months.

PG-13 MOVIES

Have you been to the movies lately? You have probably noticed that each movie has a rating. The ratings are meant to be guidelines for viewers, to explain levels of violence, language, and other characteristics of movies. The rating system was set up to prevent children from being exposed to inappropriate or intensive scenes or story lines. It seems that these days the rating is used to entice movie fans to go to a movie, as opposed to avoiding a movie.

Adding the PG-13 rating has allowed movie producers to avoid the strict standards of the ratings system. It seems that if a movie wanted to add more violence or bad language but not get the R rating, movie producers would go for the PG-13 rating. Exactly what is the difference between the R rating and the PG-13 rating? As far as I can see, there isn't one.

At one time, the R rating meant that it was not appropriate for children under a certain age. In fact, they were not allowed into the theater without an adult. Now, not only can children go to the movie without an adult, but also movie producers change the rating to PG-13 so that more kids can attend. By using the PG-13 rating, just about anything goes. When will movie executives and producers be held to a high standard again? Kids are seeing worse things on the big screen than they've ever seen before. What's next: a PG-8 rating?

STORY QUESTIONS

1. Which of the following is a reason presented in this passage as to why children should not be allowed to watch PG-13 movies?
   a. PG-13 movies are produced with higher budgets than R movies.
   b. Movie producers are allowed to add more violence and language with the PG-13 rating than an R rating.
   c. Many PG-13 movies have high levels of violence and bad language.
   d. The rating system was set up to prevent children from seeing anything inappropriate.

2. Which of the following statements would the author of this passage most likely make?
   a. Children need to be taught how to decipher the ratings system on movies.
   b. Parents should hold movie theaters accountable for letting their children in movies.
   c. Movie producers should be held to higher standards when they are given a rating for their movies.
   d. PG-13 movies should not be allowed.

3. What is the meaning of the word *intensive* as used in this passage?
   a. strenuous
   b. deceased
   c. concerned
   d. graphic

DAILY
Warm-Up 2

Name _____ Date _____

SIXTH GRADE EDUCATION

What type of school do you attend? Is it an elementary school? Is it a middle school? Or is it a junior high? Teachers throughout the country have differing opinions as to where sixth graders should go to school.

Some teachers and parents say that sixth graders should attend school in elementary schools with kindergarten through sixth grade. They feel that sixth graders are too young to go to school with seventh and eighth graders. They feel that sixth graders are still very young and impressionable. They are at a different social and emotional level than junior-highers.

Going to school with older students encourages sixth graders to behave poorly and exposes them to inappropriate behaviors. Some teachers and parents feel that sixth graders have their childhood taken away when they are in the junior high or middle school environment.

Other educators and parents feel that the needs of sixth graders would be met best in the middle school or junior high setting. In this setting, sixth graders can be encouraged and pushed to higher levels. Sixth graders in this setting can participate in school sports, and they can experience a variety of classes. They feel that keeping sixth graders in elementary school keeps them in a self-contained classroom with one teacher. Going to school with younger students keeps the sixth graders immature.

STORY QUESTIONS

1. What is the author's opinion about where sixth graders should go to school?
   a. The author thinks that sixth graders should attend elementary school.
   b. The author thinks that sixth graders should attend middle school.
   c. The author doesn't know where sixth graders should attend school.
   d. You can't tell the author's opinion from reading the passage.

2. What is the main idea of paragraph two?
   a. to explain how sixth graders adapt socially
   b. to explain the benefits of sixth graders attending elementary school
   c. to explain the benefits of sixth graders attending middle school
   d. to explain the benefits of sixth graders attending junior high school

3. Which of the following is <u>not</u> one of the reasons teachers feel that sixth graders should attend middle school?
   a. Sixth graders do not know how to switch classes.
   b. Sixth graders are too mature for the elementary school setting.
   c. Sixth graders need to be given more opportunities.
   d. Sixth graders need to be pushed to excel at a higher level.

Name _____ Date _____

SKATEBOARD PARK

There are two sides to every issue. Whether to build a skateboard park in the community is an issue that definitely has two sides. There are many people who believe the city should build a skateboard park to accommodate the number of skateboarders in the community.

This group feels that skateboarding is a new and upcoming sport and that city officials should allow skateboarders to enjoy it. The city already provides basketball courts, tennis courts, racquetball courts, and more. Among the many benefits of a skateboard park is that it would keep skateboarders off the cement driveways of banks and other public buildings. The only reason skateboarders skate there is that they have nowhere else to go.

Those with an opposing point of view feel that there should not be a public skateboard park built. The main reasons for the disapproval have to do with safety and security. A skateboard park has a reputation that comes with it. Many kids that skateboard tend to be rowdy kids who don't behave appropriately. Building a skateboard park attracts these kids, and it brings down the surrounding neighborhoods in the area.

Who would supervise the park? Many skateboarders do not wear helmets. Many fights break out at these parks. Who would be there to monitor these activities? The neighbors living nearby certainly don't want to put up with this. Finally, who will pay for the park? Cement costs a lot of money.

STORY QUESTIONS

1. Which would be the best title for this reading passage?
   a. "Choose Your Own Sports Activity"
   b. "My Community, My Choice"
   c. "Boarders vs. Non-boarders"
   d. "To Build or Not to Build"

2. Which of the following is the main reason to support a skateboard park?
   a. It will allow skateboarders a place to ride their skateboards.
   b. Parents would be more comfortable if their children were skateboarding in a park instead of in a bank driveway.
   c. The skateboarders have a right to ask the community to build them a park.
   d. The skateboarding community would be very happy.

3. What is meant by the word *reputation* as used in this passage?
   a. group restraint
   b. entitlement of a group
   c. good history
   d. belief or expectation about a group

FIX THE LIBRARY

Have you been to the school library lately? If you have, you've probably noticed that there is plenty of room for improvement. Something needs to be done to improve the school library.

The government and school leaders are all calling for better readers. They say that kids these days just don't read enough! They say they watch too much television and play too many computer games. Well, if the adults want students to read more, they need to do their part to help the kids read.

When is the last time you spent time in the school library? You've probably noticed that there isn't a very good selection of books. The number of books on the shelf is few, and the books on the shelves are old and outdated. The books have been falling apart for a long time. It is not very fun to read a book that is missing pages or is ripped or has smudge marks on it.

Not only are the books old, but they are also very outdated. There isn't a single book in the library that was written in the last 10 years. There have been so many new authors and new books that are great! Why can't the students in this school have access to these great books? The school has got to put its money where its mouth is. If they want the students to read, give them better reading material!

STORY QUESTIONS

1. People who agree with this passage probably feel that . . .
   a. parents should take more responsibility in getting books for their children.
   b. schools need to adjust their budgets to better fund the library.
   c. schools need to stop talking about the importance of reading.
   d. teachers should receive more training and instruction on how to encourage reading.

2. The main idea of this passage is . . .
   a. the library can be a great resource for students if it is funded appropriately.
   b. the school needs to have better librarians to teach students how to read.
   c. the principal should have a meeting to discuss how to improve the library.
   d. the library needs to be organized in a better manner.

3. Which statement names one of the ways suggested in the passage to improve libraries?
   a. Why can't the students in this school have access to these great books?
   b. They say that kids these days just don't read enough!
   c. If they want the students to read, give them better reading material!
   d. The number of books on the shelf is few and the books on the shelves are old and outdated.

IMPROVING RECESS

At least two or three times a day, students are released from the classroom to go to recess. Recess is meant to be a break and a time to relax the brain and release some energy. But for many students, recess is a stress and a strain. There are many things that can be done to improve recess.

First, the playground itself needs to be improved. There are too many children on the playground at one time. There just isn't enough for all the kids to do. The playground equipment is designed for about 30 children. In actuality, there are more than 100 children playing at one time.

This poses safety concerns at recess. There are too many activities going on (children running and hitting balls) to have the students so close together. There is not enough space to really play the games and activities safely. Children using the playground equipment are at risk of being injured because of such crowding. Children are also prone to fighting and arguing over the equipment, and they struggle to find things to do at recess. It is amazing that more children have not been hurt or seriously injured.

Along with these issues, there is never enough supervision for all of the children. It's impossible for one or two adults to adequately supervise 100 students at recess. Parents need to be more aware of what is taking place at recess so that they can push for improvements and changes.

STORY QUESTIONS

1. What is the main idea of the reading passage?
   a. Children enjoy free time outside.
   b. Children watch too much television.
   c. Children need more supervision.
   d. There should be changes to the way the playground is set up and supervised.

2. What is meant by the term *prone* as used in this passage?
   a. condemned
   b. uncertain
   c. more likely to
   d. excited

3. According to the passage, which of the following is a reason that playgrounds are deemed unsafe?
   a. Children are prone to fighting.
   b. The playgrounds are not constructed correctly.
   c. There is not enough cushioning beneath the playground equipment.
   d. There are too many children playing on the equipment.

SCHOOL CONDITIONS

Each year the children head back to school. Most schools open at the end of the summer months, when the heat is at its highest point. The humidity in the air only makes things worse. And what are most new students greeted with? They are greeted with a hot and sticky room that only transitions to a stiff and freezing room in a few months. Why can't schools be given adequate funds to heat and cool school buildings?

Why must students suffer the consequences of money being spent elsewhere? Children spend the greatest part of their day in the classroom. Along with poor heating and cooling, many students are attending classrooms that are old and dilapidated. Many of the schools across the nation are in terrible condition.

Many of the schools have mold growing inside the walls, along with leaks in the ceilings and walls and cracked windows and roofs. Why must our nation's children attend schools that are in such a condition? Don't they deserve the best? How do we expect them to compete with other nations when we aren't giving them the best? School districts need to look at how they are spending their money, and the state and federal governments need to ensure that the schools are given their top priority.

STORY QUESTIONS

1. What is the main idea of the first paragraph in this passage?
   a. The schools that children attend are not large enough.
   b. The schools that children attend are old and not safe.
   c. The schools that children attend do not have adequate heating and cooling.
   d. The schools that children attend do not have enough teachers.

2. What strategy does the author of the passage use to appeal to the reader?
   a. The author uses specific examples to support claims.
   b. The author uses questioning as a way to get the reader thinking.
   c. The author uses shock value to get the point across.
   d. The author uses compare and contrast as a literary technique.

3. What question shows that the author is trying to appeal to the competitive nature of parents in the audience?
   a. How do we expect them to compete with other nations when we aren't giving them the best?
   b. And what are most new students greeted with?
   c. Why can't schools be given adequate funds to heat and cool school buildings?
   d. Why must our nation's children attend school in such a condition?

Name _____

Date _____

TEACHER SALARIES

In the United States, teachers do not get paid enough. Teacher salaries have continued to be lower than they should be. In a country where education is of great worth, teachers are expected to bear the weight of teaching and educating today's children without being adequately compensated. A comment was made by a middle-school student that a convenience-store clerk makes more money than a teacher does. If the students can see the discrepancies, why can't lawmakers and other adults?

It is very difficult to attract highly qualified teachers because the best individuals have selected better-paying fields. They have chosen fields where they will be rewarded for their hard work and effort. The effects of this are that children today are falling through the cracks when it comes to their education. They are left without the skills they need to survive in today's world. They are reading and writing at low levels, and their math skills continue to decline, as well.

Some critics of raising teacher salaries state that teachers get the whole summer off and that they are paid for the time they spend on the job. This just isn't the case. Most teachers spend their summers planning and preparing for the upcoming year. Many are also attending conferences and training seminars—at their own expense—to improve their teaching abilities.

Having the summer off also puts a strain on the teacher during the school year. Teachers are highly discouraged from using "sick days" because they had all those days off in the summer. This is especially difficult for teachers who have family health issues and other problems that need their attention. Some school districts go as far as pressuring the teachers not to use sick days so that they can save money in their budgets by not using substitutes. This is wrong. Now is the time for teachers to be duly compensated for all of their hard work and effort.

STORY QUESTIONS

1. Which of the following best describes the author of this piece?
   a. reticent and quiet
   b. obnoxious and loud
   c. frustrated and demanding

2. Which statement below helps support your answer to the previous question?
   a. They are left without the skills they need to survive in today's world.
   b. This is wrong. Now is the time for teachers to be duly compensated.
   c. Teacher salaries have continued to be lower than they should be.

3. What is meant by the word *discrepancies* as used in this passage?
   a. annoyances
   b. differences
   c. challenges
   d. objectives

LUNCH CHOICES

What did you have for lunch today? Did you like your choice? When most adults go to work, they can choose from many different places to eat their lunch. Children, on the other hand, have very limited choices. This just isn't right. Children are growing and developing their bodies. They need healthy choices at every turn. They are bombarded with sweets and high-fat snacks. Providing more choices at lunch will help students grow to be healthy and strong. School administrators need to make changes.

The current choices students have now are not enough. The first choice kids have is the school cafeteria lunch. In theory, these lunches are supposed to be nutritionally sound. The reality is very different. These lunches are typically high in fat and they usually taste bad. They are bland and do not have many spices. This is done so that the meal will appeal to a large audience, but the results are boring and not very healthy.

The other choice available to students is to bring a sack lunch from home. Although this sounds like a great idea, lunches from home aren't much better. There is no refrigeration available for school lunches at school, so sack lunches are pretty limited. Usually sandwiches are the main dish. Sack lunches are typically thrown together at the last minute, and that can be a problem. They are often filled with already-packaged foods that are very high in sugar and calories. You see, this option isn't much better. There have to be more options for students to choose from at lunch so that they can have well-balanced meals at school.

STORY QUESTIONS

1. What is the main idea of this passage?
   a. Children should be given more options on what to eat for lunch.
   b. The meals in the cafeteria are bland and not appetizing.
   c. Adults have more choices than kids do for lunch.
   d. Experts disagree on the daily nutritional value of cafeteria lunches.

2. Who is the audience for this reading passage?
   a. cafeteria workers and school administrators
   b. teachers and students
   c. parents and guardians
   d. all of the above

3. Which of the following is <u>not</u> how the author describes school cafeteria lunches?
   a. bad tasting
   b. bland
   c. nutritional
   d. high in fat

DAILY Warm-Up 9

Name _____ Date _____

TOO MUCH FUNDRAISING

Every time you turn around, there seems to be another fundraiser being pushed at school. Where is the imaginary sign that reads, "Public School: Fundraising Welcome!"? It seems like every other month there is a new fundraising program taking place in the schools.

All students are pressured to participate for the good of all students. The need for fundraisers seems to be endless: new playground equipment, materials and supplies, overnight or out-of-state school trips, etc. How many tubs of cookie dough, candy, coupons, and magazines can a kid sell? Instead of getting an education, it seems that kids are getting trained to be salespeople.

The pressure tactics placed on children is also too much. Children are enticed to participate in the programs by having prizes and toys dangled in front of them. The reality is that few, if any, students actually receive any of the high-end items. It is almost impossible to sell enough items to earn the prizes promised.

Most children end up with the plastic and cheap toys. These toys are a great example of false advertising. Let's give the fundraisers a rest. Most parents would rather donate a dollar or two instead of being asked to sell another thing!

STORY QUESTIONS

1. "Children are enticed to participate in the programs by having prizes and toys dangled in front of them." *Enticed* means . . .
   a. make room for.
   b. show strength for.
   c. to compensate or adjust for.
   d. lured.

2. Which of the following is probably a reason why students feel pressured to participate in fundraisers?
   a. The school has presentations for all students, and packets are given out at school.
   b. The companies have the phone numbers of all students.
   c. Students receive grades based on their fundraising success.
   d. Teachers make sure that students are selling items door to door.

3. The passage is mostly about . . .
   a. how students are learning about false advertising.
   b. how students are learning to be salespeople.
   c. how students are pressured to get prizes.
   d. why fundraising should be kept out of school.

DAILY Name _____ Date _____

Warm-Up 10

AFTER-SCHOOL ACTIVITIES

Why don't the schools offer more after-school activities for students? Schools have the perfect set up to provide more opportunities for students to participate in healthy and meaningful activities. These activities would help keep students involved and exercising. Children do not have enough free activities available to them.

The school doesn't need to spend money to accomplish this proposal. The money has already been invested. The baseball fields and the gymnasiums in the schools should be put to good use. These facilities are not being used to their full potential. The school could easily offer activities such as baseball, basketball, volleyball, football, soccer, and running clubs.

The school could charge a nominal fee for students. The funds would go to providing a supervisor or coach. Parent volunteers could be recruited. If desired, schools could charge extra for craft, cooking, and art classes to allow more children the opportunity to participate. This proposal would not only help the children in getting their much-needed exercise, but it would also give the school a more positive image in the community.

STORY QUESTIONS

1. This passage is mostly about . . .
   a. how children are not getting enough exercise.
   b. using the school playing fields and facilities to provide more activities for kids.
   c. how the school could make more money by charging for after-school activities.
   d. whether or not schools need insurance to provide after-school activities.

2. Which of the following reasons was mentioned in the passage explaining why some people think that schools should provide after-school activities?
   a. to allow students safe places to go after school
   b. to allow a safe place for working parents to send their children after school
   c. to use the resources of playing fields and gymnasiums already built
   d. to allow schools to spend time teaching the basics during school, and to have physical education after school

3. The passage says that after-school activities would benefit the students. Which sentence supports that statement?
   a. The school could charge a nominal fee for students.
   b. Parent volunteers could be recruited.
   c. These activities would help keep students involved and exercising.
   d. If desired, schools could charge extra for craft, cooking, and art classes to allow more children the opportunity to participate.

TAKE THE TEST

Do you feel like you are constantly taking tests? It's been reported that the educators today administer more tests to students than ever before. There are tests to begin kindergarten. There are two or three achievement tests administered each year. In order to graduate from high school, students are required to take yet another test. Tests, tests, and more tests.

It's a known fact that tests are a means to determine whether or not students are learning the material being taught. However, there are many different ways to assess student comprehension and understanding. Besides, the tests seldom evaluate the information desired in the first place.

You may think that teachers are to blame for all the tests. This just isn't the case. Most teachers wish there was less testing. Did you know that many teachers are threatened if their students do not perform at a certain level on a test? They are threatened with having tenure taken away or being monitored. Teachers are also pressured to teach to the test so that students will be successful taking it. This means that important curricula and material are being ignored so that students will know how to answer questions on a test. Will knowing the answer to these test questions really make a difference in their future education or their future livelihood?

Students deserve to be taught meaningful information that will be relevant and help them excel in life. Too much time is wasted in teaching to the test. Teachers should be given more support and encouragement instead of being constantly judged on how well their students perform on various tests. All this testing has got to stop.

STORY QUESTIONS

1. What is the main idea of the third paragraph?
   a. Money should be set aside in the school budget to teach test taking skills.
   b. Parents should be held accountable for how students do on the test.
   c. The curriculum being taught in school needs to align with the test questions.
   d. Teachers should not be pressured concerning tests administered in schools.

2. Standardized tests are administered in schools with the intent to . . .
   a. determine the skills and abilities of the students.
   b. meet minimum standards set by the teachers' unions.
   c. help children become better test takers.
   d. test how well of a job the teacher is doing.

3. What does the author say will happen if the students spend too much time taking tests instead of learning valid material and subjects?
   a. Students will leave school with an insufficient education.
   b. Parents will have to start home schooling their students.
   c. The testing companies will go out of business.

SCHOOL ASSEMBLIES

Every child who attends a public school or even a private school has to deal with the idea of school assemblies. Some assemblies are put on to generate school spirit. These assemblies certainly have their place. On the other hand, there are many other school assemblies that are nothing more than a big waste of time. This practice has got to stop.

School assemblies usually turn into a punishment based on student behavior. Students are out of seats, usually sitting on the floor in a crowded room. The main feature of the assembly is usually far away, and the sound quality is very poor. No wonder students start to act up in school assemblies. It's boring, it's hard to hear, and it's uncomfortable. Heard in the background during any assembly are the harsh whispers by teachers saying, "Shhh!"

Assemblies should be optional. Students shouldn't have to participate if they wish to engage in something else—perhaps even something educational! As it is, valuable educational moments are lost while students are forced to sit through one more mind-numbing school assembly.

Students are seldom asked what type of assemblies they might find interesting. Students are never asked to share their opinions of which guest speaker they think would be interesting. Teachers need to consider the educational needs of the students before putting together one more assembly.

STORY QUESTIONS

1. What is the author's opinion of school assemblies?
   a. School assemblies are usually shallow and do not inspire students.
   b. School assemblies funny and entertaining.
   c. School assemblies are an excuse to get out of class.
   d. School assemblies are relevant and play an important role in education.

2. Which statement below from the passage portrays the author's opinion?
   a. Some assemblies are put on to generate school spirit.
   b. Students are out of seats, usually sitting on the floor in a crowded room.
   c. As it is, valuable educational moments are lost, while students are forced to sit through one more mind-numbing school assembly.
   d. Heard in the background during any assembly are harsh whispers.

3. What is meant by the statement, "Teachers need to consider the educational needs of the students before putting together one more assembly"?
   a. The author wants assemblies to be put together by the students.
   b. School assemblies can have an impact that lasts for a lifetime.
   c. School assemblies should be put together by teachers.
   d. Time spent on school assemblies shouldn't detract from the true education of the students.

DAILY Warm-Up 13 **Name** _____ **Date** _____

EMAIL MESSAGING

Most schools in the country have access to the Internet and to electronic mail. Thousands of dollars and many hours of volunteer time have been spent to ensure that this is the case. Most people agree that they want their schools to be on the cutting edge of technology. Why then, do many teachers neglect to use the resources at their fingertips?

There are many teachers who fail to communicate with parents via email. This is such a quick and easy thing to do. However, too many teachers feel that they do not have the time or the desire to be that involved technologically.

There are many benefits to having teachers communicate with parents via email on a regular basis. One of the benefits for parents is that they are able to stay up to date on missed assignments or homework that has not been turned in. Parents can also stay up to date on grades of their children. This valuable information not only helps the parents be informed, but it holds students accountable knowing that the email notices are coming home.

Email messaging is also convenient. Parents do not need to make special trips to meet with teachers. Email communication eliminates the need for both parents and teacher to try and catch each other using the phone. In many ways, email communication is also better than a parent-teacher conference! The parent is only allowed around 15 minutes per conference. That's enough time to say hello and goodbye. Email communication and other means of technological communication are the way to go!

STORY QUESTIONS

1. Which of the following are the benefits of teachers communicating with parents via email messaging?
   a. Kids are allowed to check their grades from home.
   b. Everyone has access to email.
   c. Email messaging eliminates one-on-one conflicts between teachers and parents.
   d. Email messaging allows parents and teacher to communicate about tests, grades, and homework in an effective and easy manner.

2. Which of the following is one of the reasons the author states why teachers do not use email messaging?
   a. not enough computers   c. lack of time
   b. lack of knowledge   d. no access to it

3. Which of the following could be eliminated or reduced with more communication via email messaging?
   a. student tests
   b. parent-teacher conferences
   c. curriculum nights
   d. verbal communication

DAILY Name _____ Date _____
Warm-Up 14

ROOM FOR ART

The time has come for schools to commit to the arts. School curricula have been lacking in this area for far too long. The time has come for students to be taught the arts in school. Experts have determined that teaching and involving the students in the arts is a great boost to students' self-esteem and self-image. Participation in the arts has proven to be great therapy for at-risk students.

The arts involve so many different areas. Art can be creating pottery, singing, playing an instrument, sculpting, painting a picture, tap dancing, ballet dancing, jazz dancing, poetry reading, doing mime, or acting and drama. Art is much more than just drawing a picture with crayons. Schools are missing great opportunities to reach their students by ignoring the arts. Some claim that schools can't afford to offer the arts in school. It seems apparent that schools can't afford *not* to teach the arts.

There are many different ways to incorporate the arts in the schools. There are many schools that participate in artist-in-residence programs. These programs allow professional artists to come in and share their talents and skills with the students. Artists charge nominal fees, and both the artist and the students benefit. Inviting a variety of artists allows for a variety of experiences. When finished learning about a specific art, students can share what they have learned in a performance or an exhibit.

STORY QUESTIONS

1. You can tell from the passage that the author feels that art in school leads to . . .
   a. less control of students in the school.
   b. uninspired teachers.
   c. stronger teachers and administration.
   d. educated students with a variety of experiences and opportunities.

2. Which statement from the passage portrays the author's opinion about how to bring the arts into the school?
   a. Art is much more than just drawing a picture with crayons.
   b. Inviting a variety of artists allows for a variety of experiences.
   c. Schools are missing great opportunities to reach their students by ignoring the arts.
   d. Experts have determined that teaching and involving the students in the arts is a great boost to students' self-esteem and self-image.

3. What is meant by the word *benefit* as used in the passage?
   a. advantage
   b. experience
   c. support
   d. rearranging

Name _____   **Date** _____

FEMALE SPORTS

Why isn't there more funding available for female sports? Schools across the nation spend thousands of dollars to make sure that the boys' football and basketball teams are fully funded and supported, but not much thought is put into sports for girls. It seems ridiculous that the girls' teams go without the needed equipment and coaching staff so that the boys' teams will prosper and be successful.

It's time for schools to spread the wealth. School budgets spent on boys' and girls' sports should be divided evenly. Many opponents claim that if this is done, then all support of the boys' programs will be reduced. They claim that the boys' sports programs bring in more money for the schools. But how do they know this? They've never given the girls an equal chance to compete and show their stuff.

If there were booster clubs set up for the girls' teams, then there will probably be just as much support. This is especially the case when the girls' teams are faring better than the boys' teams.

Coaches and school officials have ignored this plea for too many years. Boys' teams have coaches that are paid a much higher salary than those of the girls' teams. It's obvious that the more you spend on a position, the better and more qualified the individuals you will be able to attract.

STORY QUESTIONS

1. What is the main idea of the passage?
   a. The schools are not spending enough money on girls' sports teams.
   b. The money earned from sports programs should be returned back to the sports programs.
   c. The main idea is about whether or not the boys' sport programs have adequate funding.
   d. Parents should be responsible to provide extra money for the girls' teams and not the school.

2. You can tell from the passage that the author feels that . . .
   a. girls' sporting programs are a waste of money.
   b. girls' sporting programs need to be restructured.
   c. parents should be responsible for teaching their daughters how to play sports and not the school.
   d. girls' sports programs need better funding.

3. Which of the following statements does <u>not</u> support the author's opinion?
   a. Parents are the best supporters of the sports program.
   b. More money should be given to coaches of female teams.
   c. It is very important to allow the female sport teams to flourish.
   d. Money spent on male and female teams should be equal.

FICTION

Contemporary Realistic Fiction

Mystery/Suspense/Adventure

Historical Fiction

Fantasy

Fairy Tales/Folklore

LESSON LEARNED

Once there was young lad. He sold apples and pears at the market each day in the village. He wanted to be the first seller at the market. He knew that the earlier he got to the market, the more he could sell. It drove him crazy that other sellers always beat him. So one day, he decided that he would have to make some changes.

He decided that if he ate his breakfast at night, then he wouldn't have to eat breakfast in the morning. So that night, after he ate dinner, he ate his breakfast. He went to bed stuffed that night, but he knew it was for a good cause.

Morning came and the young lad was surprised to see that there were many people already there. He realized that his plan had failed. That night he decided to get dressed at night so he could save time in the morning. He went to bed with his work clothes on top of his pajamas. But in the morning, sellers were there before him again.

He decided to spend the night at the marketplace. He gathered up his items for sale and carried his bed to town. That night he lay on his bed and watched the night sky. The moon was full and it was hard to sleep. When morning came, the young lad was so tired that he couldn't get up. And so, he slept the day away as the buyers and sellers swirled around him.

STORY QUESTIONS

1. Which of the following events did not happen in the story?
   a. The young lad spent the night at the marketplace.
   b. The young lad ate his breakfast at night instead of in the morning.
   c. The young lad sold his spot to another man at the marketplace.

2. What can you guess about the young lad in this story?
   a. He took pity on his fellow sellers.
   b. He is very good with animals.
   c. He learned his lesson.

3. Which of the following statements is <u>not</u> true?
   a. The townspeople realized that the young lad needed a reserved spot to sell his goods.
   b. The marketplace was a busy and hectic place.
   c. Some of the sellers arrived earlier than the young lad did.

DAILY Name _____ Date _____
Warm-Up 2

CRIME DOESN'T PAY

There once was a fox that decided to rob a bank. He was tired of working at his job and knew exactly where all of the doors to the bank were located. He knew the names of all the bank tellers and when the bank opened.

The next morning, he pulled up next to the bank, slipped into his disguise, and walked up the steps of the bank. When he got to the door, the door was locked. A sign explained that the bank was closed for a holiday.

"What?" stuttered the fox. "How can the bank be closed today?"

"Today is a bank holiday," explained the doorman.

The fox stomped to his car with an angry scowl. When he got to his car, he saw a white paper blowing on his windshield.

"What is this?" roared the fox. It was a parking ticket. "How can this be?" he cried. "I can't believe I got a parking ticket!"

The fox climbed into the car, slammed on the gas pedal, and rushed into the stream of traffic. Cars had to swerve to miss the fox. The fox didn't care. He was mad. After a few moments, he looked in his rearview mirror. He screamed when he saw blue and red lights flashing. "This can't be!" said the fox. "There is no way that I will ever rob a bank. It's just too expensive."

STORY QUESTIONS

1. What is the meaning of the word *scowl* as used in this passage?
  a. curious look
  b. glare
  c. shock
  d. anger

2. After reading this story, explain how it shows that crime never pays.

  _____

  _____

  _____

3. Which sentence explains how the fox felt about his original plan?
  a. The fox also knew that his disguise would be important.
  b. The fox climbed into the car and turned on the ignition.
  c. The fox was feeling pretty good about his plan.
  d. His costume had a mask and a cape.

DAILY Name _____ Date _____
Warm-Up 3

THE LOUD RABBITS

Mother Rabbit had worked hard to make a delicious dinner for her family. She hollered for the little rabbits to come downstairs and set the table. The rabbits came down and they began to get the dishes to set the table, but they couldn't stop yelling at one another.

"I'm tired of setting the plates on the table," hollered Sister Rabbit.

"Well, it's your turn, so do it," yelled Brother Rabbit.

"Stop yelling at each other!" said Mother Rabbit. The little rabbits couldn't hear her because of their yelling, and so she shouted her demands.

After the meal was eaten, Mother Rabbit asked her "crew" to do the dishes. Again the rabbits began yelling at one another. The noise grew louder and louder. It was more than Mother Rabbit could bear.

"Stop all this yelling!" screamed Mother Rabbit. "I am tired of hearing you yell all the time!"

"Well, it's his fault!" hollered Sister Rabbit.

"No, it's not," said Brother Rabbit, not to be outdone. He yelled even louder. "If she would just do her job without bugging me. . . !" By then, Brother Rabbit had to stop and cough. His throat was getting sore from all that yelling.

"Why do you always have to yell? Why can't you just have a normal conversation? Where did you learn to yell like this?" yelled Mother Rabbit.

Suddenly the words sank into her mind, and she quietly walked up to her room. Her new-found epiphany made her stop and think.

STORY QUESTIONS

1. Which sentence shows that Mother Rabbit realized why the rabbits were yelling all the time?
   a. Suddenly the words sank into her mind and she quietly walked up to her room.
   b. His throat was getting sore from all that yelling.
   c. Again the rabbits began yelling at one another.
   d. Mother Rabbit had worked hard to make a delicious dinner for her family.

2. What is the meaning of the word *epiphany* as used in the story?
   a. recruitment
   b. turn
   c. understanding
   d. arrangement

3. What is the moral to the story?
   a. Never count your eggs before they hatch.
   b. Do unto others as you want done to yourself.
   c. Don't bite the hand that feeds you.

HOUSE GUESTS

There once was a chicken, a duck, and a goose. The three animals were the best of friends. They did everything together.

One morning, Duck awoke in a very good mood. He decided to invite his friends Chicken and Goose over for lunch. He called his friends and extended the invitation. They both accepted. Then Duck began making a delicious lunch. He got fresh grain from the bin and berries from the patch. He was determined to make this a lunch that would not soon be forgotten.

When the clock struck 12, the doorbell rang. Duck quickly ran to the door to greet his guests. He invited Chicken and Goose in with a flourish. Before long, lunch was served, and Duck was pleased with the response. Chicken and Goose loved the food. Each and every bite was delicious. When the meal was finished, all three animals sat down to visit on the back porch.

As time went by, Duck began to yawn. He was tired. He had spent his whole morning making lunch and now he was ready for his nap. He dropped hint after hint, but the two would not leave.

Finally, Duck got up and went inside. He locked the door. He left his guests outside alone. Surprised, Goose and Chicken got up and started for home.

"He sure is a rude host," commented Chicken.

"He sure is," said Goose, and they hurried on down the path.

STORY QUESTIONS

1. What does the word *flourish* mean in the story?
   a. without interest   c. excited gesture
   b. separately   d. organized

2. Which paragraph contains Duck's response to his friends not leaving?
   a. third paragraph   c. fifth paragraph
   b. second paragraph   d. sixth paragraph

3. Which of the following would make a good title for the story?
   a. "The Impolite Guests"
   b. "Chicken and Goose"
   c. "House Visit"
   d. "Lunch with Tea"

4. What is the moral to the story?
   a. Do not wear out your welcome.
   b. Wash your hands before dinner.
   c. Too many cooks spoil the broth.
   d. Crime doesn't pay.

Name _____ **Date** _____

LAZY BONES

There once was a farmer who worked hard. He was always cold or always sunburned. It was a hard life, but he never complained.

The farmer had two sons. Both sons were lazier than any other sons. The farmer was saddened by the attitude of his sons. But try as he might, he was not able to convince the boys to do anything different.

"How can I teach my boys to work hard?" he thought. "This farm has been part of our family for many generations. Each man has worked hard on the farm, but my sons seem more content to play and be lazy."

The farmer pondered his problem. He just didn't know what to do. Day in and day out, the farmer invited the sons to come help him work, but each day they declined and sat around playing card games and drinking root beer.

"I will soon die," said the farmer one day. "A treasure has been buried somewhere on the farm. But I have not been able to find it. When I die, will you try to find it?"

The sons agreed, and the farmer soon died. The sons immediately began digging up the farm. They were eager to find the treasure. In all their digging they were able to overturn the soil and keep it moist. The farm did better than it ever had done, but the treasure was never found. Some say that to this day, the sons are still digging.

STORY QUESTIONS

1. Where in the story is the conflict stated?
   a. second paragraph
   b. end of the first paragraph
   c. end of the third paragraph
   d. beginning of the first paragraph

2. What is the conflict of this story?
   a. The farmer doesn't know how to plant the right crops for his farm.
   b. The farmer doesn't know who to pass his farm onto when he dies.
   c. The farmer's sons are lazy and won't work.
   d. The sons have not been taught how to care for themselves.

3. What is the meaning of the word *declined* as used in the story?
   a. rejected
   b. offended
   c. decided
   d. accepted

DAILY Name _____ Date _____
Warm-Up 6

STICK TOGETHER

There once were four bulls that lived in a field. They were only concerned about one thing. Occasionally, a lion would creep around the field stalking them. The bulls were worried that the lion would kill them, and so they had a discussion about what they should do.

One of the bulls suggested that they attack the lion and kill him. But the other bulls agreed that the lion was much stronger than any one of them and was a much better fighter, as well.

Another bull suggested that they talk to the lion to see if he would leave them alone. But the other three bulls disagreed. The lion didn't care about their desires. He only wanted to eat them.

Finally, the third bull suggested that they work together to save themselves from the lion. He suggested that each time the lion came to the field, they should stand back to back. That way, anywhere the lion went, he would be met with heavy horns and a strong kick from the legs. All bulls agreed that this was a great plan.

The next day, the lion came sauntering through the field. The bulls quickly got in their circle. No matter where the lion attacked, he was met with kicks and horns.

The plan worked until one day the bulls got in a fight. They each went to a corner of the field. When the lion came to make his attack, he got each of the bulls without a struggle.

STORY QUESTIONS

1. What is the moral to the story?
   a. Birds of a feather flock together.
   b. One for all, and all for one.
   c. United we stand, divided we fall.
   d. Don't judge a book by its cover.

2. What is the meaning of the word *sauntered* as used in the story?
   a. poked
   b. strolled
   c. directed
   d. ran

3. Explain how the moral to this story fits. Why were the bulls vulnerable to an attack from the lion?

   _____

   _____

   _____

   _____

WELL SAID

Henry the badger was the youngest member of his family. He often felt ignored and tried to get attention by the things he said.

"You are looking bigger today than you ever have," said Henry to his sister. His sister left the den crying.

Later in the day, Henry told his brother that the picture he drew in the sand looked ugly. The brother ran in to the den crying. Henry sat on the rock and wondered what he should do next. Just then, Henry's mom came strolling over.

"I need you to put this sock in your mouth," Mother said.

"A sock in my mouth? Why?" asked Henry

Just then, Henry's mother stuffed the sock in Henry's mouth. He let out a gargled cry.

Later in the afternoon, Henry saw his Aunt Bertie walking up with a loaf of bread. "Oh, yuck," thought Henry. "Her bread is always so disgusting!" He was about to say that when he choked on the sock that was still in his mouth. Henry's aunt smiled and walked right on past him.

That night, while Henry's family was having dinner, Henry was about to tattle on his older brother for something, but ended up gagging on the sock. Henry's mother smiled at him. Henry looked into his mother's eyes and began to understand the lesson she was trying to teach him.

That same night, he wrote a letter to his mom asking for permission to remove the sock, and he promised to watch his words. His mother winked as Henry took out the sock.

STORY QUESTIONS

1. What is the lesson in this story?
   a. What goes around comes around.
   b. If you can't say anything nice, don't say anything at all.
   c. A rolling stone gathers no moss.
   d. No use crying over spilt milk.

2. What would be a good title for this reading passage?
   a. "Henry Learns a Lesson"   c. "The Leader of the Pack"
   b. "Henry vs. the Family"   d. "Them Is Fightin' Words"

3. Locate the statement below that is <u>not</u> true.
   a. Henry seemed insecure about himself and so he took it out on others.
   b. Henry didn't say very nice things to his family members.
   c. Henry's mother put a sock in Henry's mouth.
   d. Henry was learning to ride his bike.

Fiction: Fairy Tales/Folklore

Name _____ **Date** _____

PEER PRESSURE

A group of squirrels lived in the branches of the great cottonwood tree on Farmer Jack's farm. The squirrels had lived there for many years and had built up a great home nestled in the tree. Sammy always seemed to be looking for adventure.

One day, Sammy saw a trap that the farmer had set. Most of the squirrels knew that they should avoid the traps. Sammy slowly walked up to the trap and sniffed it. As he left, his tail brushed over the trap. Snap! Sammy's tail had gotten caught in the trap! It had cut Sammy's big bushy tail right off! He gasped, "Yikes! My tail! What am I going to do?"

That night at dinner, Sammy sulked as he ate his food. He was so sad about his tail that he just didn't know what to do.

The next morning, Sammy got up early. He planned to visit all the squirrels he could find. While visiting with the squirrels, he encouraged each of them to cut off their tails. He explained the benefits of doing so and modeled his own stub. Each squirrel considered his request, but in the end told Sammy that they liked their tails.

One squirrel wisely said, "Sammy, just because you lost your tail over foolishness does not mean we should join you." Sammy slowly made his way home. He would have dragged his tail between his legs if he had one.

STORY QUESTIONS

1. What is the main conflict or problem in this story?
   a. Sammy always seems to be looking for adventure, and this time he gets into trouble.
   b. Sammy was trying to convince the other squirrels to be like him so that he wouldn't feel so badly.
   c. Sammy got his tail cut off.
   d. Sammy was not successful at making the other squirrels cut their tails off.

2. What is the meaning of the word *sulked* as used in the story?
   a. chilly
   b. frantic
   c. disrupted
   d. moped

3. What is the moral to this story?
   a. A bird in the hand is better than three in a bush.
   b. A friend in need is a friend indeed.
   c. Work before play.
   d. Misery loves company.

THE LONG JUMP

Frieda the goat loved to go to the well. Each day she stopped to get a long drink. On this particular day, she could hear noises coming from the well. She went to the well to see what was inside.

What she saw down in the well caught her by surprise. There was a wolf. He was so big that he could barely fit inside the well.

"What are you doing?" asked Frieda.

"Getting a drink," replied the frustrated wolf.

"But why did you get inside the well to get the drink?" asked Frieda.

"Oh, it's much easier this way," lied the wolf. "Besides, I can get a much bigger drink down here."

"Oh," answered Frieda, and she waited patiently for her turn. After a few minutes, the wolf asked Frieda if she wouldn't mind helping him out of the well. Frieda thought about it for a minute and decided that she should help. The wolf told her to climb inside the well and then he would step on her back to get out.

"But then how will I get out myself?" asked Frieda.

"We'll figure something out," replied the wolf.

Frieda climbed down into the well, and the wolf stepped on her back to get out. The wolf disappeared and Frieda hollered, "Hey! Aren't you going to help me?"

The wolf came back and peered down into the well. "You foolish goat! You should have never jumped down into the well." And with that, he hurried off into the forest.

STORY QUESTIONS

1. What is the problem in the story?
   a. Frieda is thirsty and needs a drink.
   b. The wolf is stuck down in the well.
   c. Frieda gets stuck in the well trying to help the wolf.
   d. Frieda no longer wants to help the wolf.

2. Which one of the following words best describes the wolf?
   a. unhappy   c. conniving
   b. insecure   d. tall

3. What is the moral to the story?
   a. Look before you leap.
   b. A friend in need is a friend indeed.
   c. Work before play.
   d. none of the above

DAILY Warm-Up 10 Name _____ Date _____

PRETTY SONG

One sunny afternoon, a crow swooped down and gathered a piece of meat in its mouth. A lion had watched the whole thing happen, and he was jealous of the crow. He wanted the piece of meat in the worst way. He was hungry and started to drool. He thought and thought about what he could do to get the meat from the crow. Finally, he had an idea.

He sat down at the foot of the tree and called up to the crow, "Hey, crow, don't your feathers look crisp and clean today?" The crow smiled to himself and admired his feathers.

The lion then said, "Hey, crow, your beak looks awfully handsome today, as well." The crow smiled again and felt his face turning red.

At this point, the lion knew that the crow was probably ready for the next step. He called out, "Hey, crow, I've heard you have a beautiful voice. Do you mind singing just a few notes for me?"

By this time, the crow was beaming. He knew his voice was beautiful. He immediately opened his mouth and let out a shrill sound. The notes cascaded down to the base of the tree. The piece of meat that was in the crow's mouth fell out. It landed at the lion's feet. The lion snatched up the meat and scurried off into the forest.

STORY QUESTIONS

1. What lesson did the crow probably learn in the story?
   a. Good things come in small packages.
   b. Birds of a feather flock together.
   c. Flatterers are not to be trusted.
   d. A bird in hand is better than three in the bush.

2. What is meant by the meaning of the word *cascaded*?
   a. fell
   b. slumped
   c. defended
   d. swaggered

3. Which sentence below is not true?
   a. The crow was flattered by the lion's kind words.
   b. The crow was able to get a piece of meat.
   c. The crow grew tired of listening to the lion.
   d. The crow dropped the meat to the lion.

4. Which of the following animals was <u>not</u> in the story?
   a. lion
   b. hen
   c. crow

Name _____   Date _____

THE JEALOUS WOLF

There once was a wolf that spent his day catching rabbits. He prided himself in catching the biggest and fattest ones around. One morning he spotted the perfect rabbit. He proceeded to chase it. The rabbit was quick. He was able to dodge the wolf for a very long time. However, the rabbit soon tired and was caught by the wolf.

The wolf was tired and headed for home. As he crossed the bridge, he happened to look down into river. He was amazed at what he saw. There standing in the river was another wolf. This wolf had a rabbit in his mouth, as well, but it looked much bigger.

This made the wolf angry. He was known for his hunting skills, and he always caught the biggest rabbit. How dare this wolf try to outdo him! As the wolf continued to trot along, he couldn't stand it any longer. He ran back to the edge of the bridge and looked down at the wolf with the bigger rabbit. He wanted that rabbit instead of the one in his mouth. Without a moment of hesitation, he plunged over the side of the bridge. The rabbit in his own mouth fell into the water and sank to the bottom of the river.

Once the wolf jumped into the river, he couldn't find the other wolf anywhere. He sputtered around looking, but the other wolf was never found. The wolf, saddened by the loss of his rabbit, went home hungry.

STORY QUESTIONS

1. What was the wolf in the river?
   a. The wolf in the river was a cousin to the wolf on the bridge.
   b. The wolf in the river was just his imagination.
   c. The wolf in the river was just a reflection of himself.
   d. none of the above.

2. What lesson did the wolf learn?
   a. A rolling stone gathers no moss.
   b. Pride goes before the fall.
   c. Practice makes perfect.
   d. The early bird gets the worm.

3. Which of the following statements can be determined after reading the passage?
   a. The wolf was prideful.
   b. The wolf was scared.
   c. The wolf was not a good swimmer.
   d. The wolf was content with what he had.

DAILY
Warm-Up 12

Name _____   Date _____

THE OLD MAN'S DAUGHTERS

There once was an old man who had three daughters. The daughters were each very beautiful and talented. Each day, the old man would try to wake his daughters to help him on the farm. But each day only the youngest daughter would rise from her bed to help her father.

The old man wished he could think of a way to get his two oldest daughters to rise from their beds so they could learn to work. But try as he might, he could not convince them. He secretly devised a plan. Late that night, he buried a diamond ring in the cabbage patch.

Early the next morning, he woke his three daughters, but only the youngest got up. She went to work in the cabbage patch. Imagine her surprise when she came across the diamond ring! The other daughters were furious. They didn't think it was fair.

The next night, the old man buried a diamond necklace in the apple orchard. The following morning, the youngest daughter found the necklace as she picked apples. The other daughters were outraged.

But the old man's plan worked. Early the third morning, all three daughters arose when called and went to work. They worked all day, but they never found anything special. They continued getting up each morning hoping to find a surprise. The old man smiled to himself. His plan had worked. With a twinkle in his eye, he set about his work.

STORY QUESTIONS

1. What is the moral of this story?
   a. What goes around comes around.
   b. Work before play.
   c. A rolling stone gathers no moss.
   d. The early bird gets the worm.

2. What would be a good title for this reading passage?
   a. "Patience Is a Virtue"
   b. "The Two Sleepyheads"
   c. "Work Before Play"
   d. "Commitment Has Its Reward"

3. Locate the statement below that is <u>not</u> a fact.
   a. Two of the daughters slept in late every morning.
   b. The old man was concerned about his daughters' work ethic.
   c. The old man was trying to punish his daughters by making them work late.
   d. The oldest daughters were upset with the youngest daughter.

Name _____ **Date** _____

CLIMBING HIGH

Each morning, Kinga the koala bear would get up to practice climbing trees. She wanted to compete in the annual tree-climbing contest. Her mother didn't think she was big enough. Her father didn't think she was strong enough. Her friends didn't think she was tough enough. But Kinga had the will to try.

There were other races around the area that Kinga decided to compete in before the big event. At her first race, Kinga came in dead last. Tears dropped from her eyes as she walked home. She knew that she could have done better, but she had forgotten to get her claws deep enough inside the tree because she was so worried about going fast. The onlookers laughed at her as she slipped down the tree.

At the next small race, Kinga dug her claws in so deep that she had a hard time getting them out fast enough. In fact, Kinga was stuck for a few minutes. The crowd laughed as Kinga came in last again.

Finally, the day of the annual tree-climbing event was here. Kinga's parents were so worried about their daughter. They didn't want her to be laughed at again! But as the whistle blew, Kinga raced up the tree. She was the first to reach the top. She had won! She couldn't believe it. The crowd cheered for Kinga. As Kinga walked home at the end of the day, a tear trickled down her face—but this time it was a tear of joy!

STORY QUESTIONS

1. What is the problem in the story?
   a. Kinga's mom thinks that she isn't big enough.
   b. Kinga's father thinks that she isn't strong enough.
   c. The crowd is laughing at Kinga.
   d. Kinga is having a hard time learning how to climb the tree quickly.

2. Which of the following words best describes Kinga?
   a. dedicated
   b. insecure
   c. quick-witted
   d. dull

3. What is the moral to the story?
   a. People in glass houses shouldn't throw stones.
   b. If at first you don't succeed, try, try again.
   c. Big things come in small packages.
   d. Don't put all of your eggs in one basket.

DAILY
Warm-Up 14

Name _____ Date _____

GOOD FORTUNE

There once was a young tortoise walking through the desert. It had been a dry year, and the drought was taking its toll on the animals. The tortoise had searched in vain for food. On this day, things had been especially tough. The tortoise was about to give up and stopped next to a large rock to rest.

"Oh, how I wish I could eat some food," said the tortoise.

The tortoise looked down and saw something very unusual. Sticking out from the rock was a pile of leaves. The tortoise walked around to the other side of the rock and was stunned to see a large pile of leaves, lettuce, berries, and more.

"What good fortune I have in finding this food. Now I will not starve to death," said the tortoise as he sat down to eat.

It didn't take long before the tortoise was joined by an old tortoise. The old tortoise looked longingly at the food. The younger tortoise did not want to share his food. Minute by minute the time ticked away and the old tortoise continued to stare at the young tortoise eating his food. The young tortoise couldn't handle it any longer and so he said, "Would you like some of this food?"

"I would love that," said the old tortoise.

Before long, the two tortoises were munching away. The young tortoise had a good feeling inside. He was glad he had decided to share his food. Somehow he didn't seem as hungry anymore.

STORY QUESTIONS

1. What was the lesson learned in this story?
   a. Patience is a virtue.
   b. Sharing is caring.
   c. People in glass houses shouldn't throw stones.
   d. A watched pot never boils.

2. How does the tortoise learn his lesson?
   a. He gets in a fight with the tortoise.
   b. He takes advantage of the old tortoise.
   c. He teaches by example.
   d. He begins to feel badly and shares his good fortune.

3. Using the context clues, what is the meaning of the word *toll*?
   a. price   c. anger
   b. worry   d. lane

PLAN B

A fox and a cat were having an argument about who was best at being able to free himself from danger. The cat explained that he had an easy way to escape. He would climb a tree. The fox claimed that he had at least 10 means of escape: he could fight, hide in a den, run fast, and so on.

Just then, a pack of dogs could be heard in the distance. Both the cat and the fox were scared. They knew that the pack of dogs would eat them if given the chance. The cat quickly scampered up the tree. He knew he would be safe there.

The fox, on the other hand, couldn't decide what to do. First, he ran to his den to hide. Then he jumped up and ran to the river; he would swim faster than the dogs. But that would not work. He decided to run faster than them. The poor fox didn't know what to do. As he scurried around from one option to another, he grew tired.

Before long, the dogs were there. The fox began to run, but he was exhausted. He was worn out and couldn't stay far enough ahead of the dogs. It didn't take long before the dogs overtook him, and that was the end of the fox.

The cat in the tree watched the whole thing.

He shook his head and said to himself, "That poor fox. He should have gone with just one of his plans!"

STORY QUESTIONS

1. What is the moral to the story?
   a. Birds of a feather flock together.
   b. Better one safe way than a hundred you cannot choose between.
   c. Practice makes perfect.
   d. Don't judge a book by its cover.

2. What is the meaning of the word *scurried* as used in the passage?
   a. astonished
   b. confused
   c. ignored
   d. dashed

3. Which of the following statements can be verified from the story?
   a. The fox was afraid of the cat and the dogs.
   b. The fox and the dogs had been in a fight before.
   c. The fox had a hard time making decisions.
   d. The fox and the dogs were going to put on a show for the cat.

DAILY
Warm-Up 16

Name _____ Date _____

TRUE LOVE

There once was an old man and an old woman. They had been married for 50 years. By this time in life, they had grown tired of each other. They fought day and night. The old man had tired of this practice and decided that it needed to stop.

He went to see the wise man of the village to ask his advice. The wise man counseled the old man to leave for two days. The old man did as he was told, but he didn't understand. After two days, he returned home, only to hear his wife complain about his absence and all the work she had to do while he was gone.

The old man sought the wise man's advice again, who this time told the old man to leave for a week. And so, the old man packed his bags and left for a week. Upon his return, his wife complained bitterly.

The old man was about to give up, but he went to the wise man again begging for advice. The wise man told the old man to leave for a month. The old man was about to protest, but left instead.

Upon his return, the wife ran to greet him and threw her arms around him. She had missed him so much. She never wanted him to leave again. The old man wondered what had happened, but he wasn't about to question his good fortune. He hugged the old woman and began unpacking his suitcase.

STORY QUESTIONS

1. What did the old man learn from this experience?
   a. Do not put all your eggs in one basket.
   b. Good things come to those who wait.
   c. Absence makes the heart grow fonder.
   d. Work before play.

2. From reading the story, which of the following words could be used to describe the wise man?
   a. poor
   b. clever
   c. arrogant
   d. simple

3. Why did the wife change her feelings about the old man?

_____

_____

_____

FIRE ON THE PRAIRIE

The smoke came pouring out of the barn all at once. It seemed that the fire started immediately and went from bad to worse. It took a while for the smoke to reach the noses of the Steed family inside the house. Pa had just sat down to say grace over the meal when he smelled the smoke. He jumped out of his seat. At the same moment, Joe yelled, "Fire!"

Mother gathered her skirts about her and ran to get a bucket. Mimi shuddered as she looked at her family in a panic. She grabbed Baby Ellie, who had started crying from all the commotion, and she ran outside. The smoke was thick, and the barn was engulfed in flames.

"If we hurry, maybe we can save part of it," called Pa.

Joe was throwing buckets of water as quickly as he could, but they didn't seem to have any effect. Mimi could see his muscles bulging through his shirt. Mother was hitting the flames with a large rug.

Just then, a wagon pulled up and Mimi saw the Jenkins who lived just down the way, jump out and rush over to help. They must have seen the flames from a distance. The Jenkins had five sons. Their help came at the perfect time. The fire that once seemed formidable was reduced to a small flame.

"Thanks," gasped Pa to the Jenkins. "I owe you one."

"Happy to help," said the oldest Jenkins boy as he climbed back into the wagon.

STORY QUESTIONS

1. Which sentence contains evidence that the story takes place during the time the settlers set up homes on the prairies?
   a. At the same moment, Joe yelled, "Fire!"
   b. "If we hurry, maybe we can save part of it," called Pa.
   c. Mother gathered her skirts about her and ran to get a bucket.
   d. Just then, a wagon pulled up and Mimi saw the Jenkins family jump out.

2. Where in the story does it explain the problem?
   a. first paragraph
   b. second paragraph
   c. third paragraph
   d. fourth paragraph

3 Which of the following characters did <u>not</u> have a speaking part in the story?
   a. Pa
   b. Joe
   c. Mimi
   d. the oldest Jenkins boy

4. What is the meaning of the word *formidable* as used in the story?
   a. fearsome
   b. poor quality
   c. annoying

DAILY
Warm-Up 2

Name _____ Date _____

FIRM IN THE FAITH

Faith had immigrated to America with her family three years ago. She loved adventure, and this had definitely been one. She had grown to love her new home and all its surroundings.

Times were tough for the colonists. They had been waging a war for independence against the British. Faith's father had gone to fight with the great George Washington. Washington was a legend in Faith's family, but especially in her mind. She dreamed of meeting him, but she knew that her chances were slim, for he was a busy man.

The day began with the normal chores and routine. Faith cleaned out the fireplace and got a wood stack for the midday meal. She was picking apples in the orchard when her mother called and asked her to take a letter to town. Faith scurried down the tree and headed towards town with the letter tucked inside her apron.

As she got closer to the town, she could see a commotion. A shot of fear raced down her back. What if it were the British? She could see a crowd gathered, and she pushed her way to the front. There, in the center of the crowd, was a man on a horse. It was none other than General Washington himself. People pushed Faith out of the way, but not before Faith saw him wink in her direction. Faith ran the whole way home to share her unbelievable story. Her heart pounded as she ran up the steps of the house.

STORY QUESTIONS

1. Which of the following sentences does not show when the story takes place?
   a. Faith had immigrated to America with her family three years ago.
   b. Times were tough for the colonists.
   c. She loved adventure, and this had definitely been one.
   d. They had been waging a war for independence against the British.

2. What is the meaning of the word *slim* as used in the story?
   a. thin
   b. small
   c. timid
   d. frail

3. Which of the following statements was <u>not</u> mentioned in the story?
   a. Faith cleaned out the fireplace and got a wood stack for the midday meal.
   b. Faith rode her horse quickly into town to meet General Washington.
   c. She was picking apples in the orchard when her mother called . . .
   d. People pushed Faith out of the way, but not before Faith saw him wink in her direction.

DAILY Name _____ Date _____
Warm-Up 3

FACE TO FACE

For as long as Matthew could remember, he had been walking behind a wagon. Day in and day out, Matthew had walked and walked and walked. He was ready to be done with the journey.

Each day at dusk, the wagon train would bring the wagons into a circle. This formation served as a shield of protection. Members of the wagon train were encouraged to stay inside the circle at all times. But tonight, Matthew was tired. He was tired of doing the same thing every day. Tonight he would sneak away right after dinner just to get some air.

Finally, it was time. Matthew walked so far away that he could barely hear the adults singing songs around the campfire. He squatted down against a rock and leaned back to look at the night sky. Matthew closed his eyes.

Suddenly, his eyes flickered open, and standing directly above him was the biggest wolf that Matthew had ever seen. Matthew's body began to quake with fear. He slowly got up. He didn't know what else to do, so he started edging his way back to the wagons. The wolf followed him the whole way.

Just then, Matthew heard a gunshot and watched the wolf fall at his feet. He turned to see his father standing a ways off. He ran to the safety of his father's arms. He knew that would be the last time he ever stepped out of the wagon circle again.

STORY QUESTIONS

1. What is the meaning of the word *edging* as used in this passage?
   a. binding up
   b. moving closer
   c. closing up
   d. along the perimeter

2. Which sentence shows how Matthew feels about his dad's help?
   a. He was tired of doing the same thing every day.
   b. He started etching his way back to the wagons.
   c. He had been walking behind a wagon.
   d. He ran to the safety of his father's arms.

3. Which paragraph shows the resolution to the problem in the passage?
   a. second paragraph
   b. fifth paragraph
   c. fourth paragraph
   d. first paragraph

A GOOD BOOK

Nellie lived with her family on a large plantation. The plantation had been in the family for generations. Nellie's father owned slaves—hundreds of them. Because of the hard work of the slaves, Nellie's family was very successful.

Nellie loved to read, and as a result, books were strewn throughout the house. Nellie's nanny, Winifred, a black slave who had cared for Nellie since birth, spent most of her time picking up books after Nellie. Nellie was enthralled with books.

That afternoon, Nellie had left a book on the kitchen counter and slipped off to play with her friend, Rose. Rose was Winifred's daughter, and they were the same age.

"What do you want to do today?" asked Rose with a smile.

"I know exactly what we're going to do," replied Nellie. "I'm going to teach you to read."

"But I'm not allowed to read," cautioned Rose.

"Says who?" asked Nellie. "You've got to read. It's very important."

The girls sat in the window seat, and Nellie began to show Rose the alphabet. Just then, Nellie's father entered the room. He couldn't believe what he saw. "Nellie, what in tarnation are you doing?" hollered her father. "You know slaves aren't supposed to read!"

"Why not, father?" asked Nellie. "What's wrong with reading?"

"Well, nothing is wrong with reading. It's just that . . ."

Nellie quickly put her hand to her father's face. "Then let's continue our lesson," interrupted Nellie. "Rose, say it again," she continued, and her father walked out of the room.

STORY QUESTIONS

1. Why did Nellie's father think that it wasn't right for Nellie to teach Rose to read?

   _____

   _____

2. What does the word *enthralled* mean?
   a. opposite
   b. enchanted
   c. partnership with
   d. opened up

3. After reading the passage, what is a word that could be used to describe Nellie?
   a. careless
   b. forgetful
   c. spirited
   d. mean

A SAFE LANDING

Jacob's family had just staked the claim for the land two weeks before. They were clearing the land of trees to begin their crops. Jacob and his pa had been working long days to accomplish the task.

Thanks to Old Blue, the job was a bit easier. As each tree was cut down, Pa would attach a chain to the horse, and Old Blue would help pull the large stump out of the dirt.

"Let's do one more, Jake," encouraged Pa. "That way, the first section will be done."

Pa attached the chain once and stepped back to allow Old Blue to do her job. Jacob slowly got to his feet and began pushing the log. Every muscle in his body was taut and aching. The stump started to budge.

Just then, a loud SNAP could be heard. As if in slow motion, Jacob saw the chain break free from the horse and fly toward his father. Jacob lunged at his father, knocking him to the ground. Jacob lay on top of his father panting. Sweat dripped from his face, and he peered into the eyes of his father. Pa turned his head to hide the tear that was trickling down the side of his face, but Jacob saw it.

"Thanks, Jake," said Pa quietly. "I can't thank you enough."

"No problem, Pa," replied Jacob. "Why don't we call it a day?"

"Great idea," said Pa as he hugged his boy. And yet, this boy seemed more like a man.

STORY QUESTIONS

1. Why was Jacob shoving his Pa to the ground?
    a. Jacob could see that the chain was going to hit him.
    b. Jacob was upset that they had to pull one more tree stump.
    c. Jacob was trying to keep his dad from getting run over by the horse.
    d. Jacob slipped and landed on his Pa.

2. What is the main idea of the second paragraph?
    a. to explain how Old Blue slipped and the chain broke
    b. to explain the relationship between Jacob and his Pa
    c. to explain the process of how they were getting the stumps out of the ground
    d. to explain the mannerisms of Old Blue

3. What is the meaning of the word *taut* in the fourth paragraph?
    a. loose
    b. strained
    c. bothered
    d. squirmed

THE CHRISTMAS GIFT

Anna smiled as her little brother and sister each opened a gift left by Santa Claus. It had been a rough year for the Sorensen family. Father had worked hard to get a claim on land on the western side of Minnesota. The family had traveled from England to make a new start in America. The trip on the boat had been long and depressing. Everyone got sick; and Anna, who was the healthiest of the family, spent her time caring for the family.

Upon their arrival in America, the Sorensens had a hard time finding their trunks and belongings. It took three weeks before they were ready to leave New York. Mother was very sick during this time, and Anna worried about her constantly.

Once the luggage had been secured and Father made arrangements to travel to their land, they set off for Minnesota. Mother continued to worsen, and Anna took on all of her mother's roles. She cared for her mother in the back of the wagon. Day in and day out, her mother had a fever.

It all came to an end one morning when Anna came back from a spring with fresh water.

"Mama!" shrieked Anna. She saw her mother's slumped body leaning in the wagon. But it was too late: she was dead. The months that followed were filled with tears and grief. The summer months turned to fall, and soon winter was upon the family.

Anna's thoughts turned back to the present and Christmas morning. Just then, Father handed her a gift. Anna was surprised. She didn't expect to receive anything this Christmas. She started to protest.

"Open it," interrupted Father. Anna opened the gift and saw her mother's shawl.

"I just can't," said Anna softly.

"You must. Mother would have wanted you to have it," said Father. "You've worked so hard to care for our family. You deserve it."

STORY QUESTIONS

1. What is the main idea of paragraph two?
   a. The family had a difficult time getting to Minnesota because of delays.
   b. The family did not receive the land claim they desired.
   c. Mother was trying to get well, but not much could be done.
   d. Anna opened her Christmas gift and felt she couldn't take it.

2. Which of the following sentences portrays the problem in this story?
   a. Anna and her siblings didn't have Christmas gifts.
   b. After the death of her mother, Anna doesn't feel she can take her shawl.
   c. The Sorensens didn't have any heat in the winter.
   d. Anna's father is upset he doesn't have any Christmas gifts.

3. Which of the following did not happen in the story?
   a. Anna takes on the burden of caring for her family.
   b. Anna's little sister is sick and never recovers.
   c. Anna's father insisted that she take her mother's shawl.
   d. Anna' family lost their trunks and luggage.

THE SUBSTITUTE

The students in the one-room schoolhouse had learned long ago that they were in charge. The students were unruly and impossible to manage. They were proud of the fact that they had run all 10 of their intended teachers out of the position so far that year. That was until Mrs. Snyder arrived.

Mrs. Snyder walked up the steps with an air about her. She had arrived at school long before the children got there so that she could get the fire burning in the fireplace. As the students filed into the room, it was warm and toasty.

When it came time to pull the slates out of the wooden box by the board, the boys held their breath, waiting to hear her scream when she saw the mouse. But she didn't scream: she picked it up and threw it out the open window.

Deflated, the kids resigned themselves to completing the lesson. Mrs. Snyder had a way of making things interesting and entertaining. Before they knew it, it was lunchtime.

At the end of the day, Mrs. Snyder thanked the students for their hospitality. She explained that she was the substitute called to teach for just one day. The students looked stunned.

"Mrs. Snyder, you've got to stay," cried Joey. "You're the best teacher I've ever had."

"That's right," added Missy.

"Please stay!" the students chanted.

"Oh, alright! If you insist," said Mrs. Snyder with a twinkle in her eye, and she began unpacking her bag.

STORY QUESTIONS

1. Which of the following statements is <u>not</u> true in the story?
   a. Mrs. Snyder decides to remain a substitute teacher.
   b. Mrs. Snyder made the students get their work done.
   c. The students were surprised when Mrs. Snyder said she was a substitute.
   d. The students learn to appreciate Mrs. Snyder and pay her respect.

2. Which of the following words could be used to describe Mrs. Snyder?
   a. angry
   b. clever
   c. misguided
   d. overly excitable

3. What is the meaning of the word *resigned* as used in the passage?
   a. intuitive and inspired
   b. overbearing and rude
   c. sadly accepted
   d. instrumental in making change

DAILY
Warm-Up 8

Name _____ Date _____

HERDING CATTLE

Hannah and Henry were born two minutes apart. Since that time, they had seldom been separated. Today was no different. The two had been given the assignment of rounding up the herd of cattle.

The twins lived with their parents on a large ranch in Texas. Generations of their family had run cattle across the many miles for many years. Their grandfather had fought in the Mexican-American War. They were proud of their land and freedom.

"C'mon, Hannah," yelled Henry. "Let's go. The cows are starting to head for the wash."

"I'm trying," barked Hannah. The day was hot and sticky.

Just then, a cow with a big head of sharp horns raced to a stop in front of Hannah. Dust billowed into the air. The cow stood panting as if daring Hannah to move. Hannah let out a whimper. "Henry?"

"Come on!" yelled Henry. He turned to look back at his sister. He was surprised to find the whole herd lined up in front of Hannah. "Wow," said Henry, whispering this time. "Walk as slowly as you can out of the way. They're just trying to pass."

Hannah slowly stepped out of the way. After a few minutes, the cattle began shuffling their way towards the corral. Henry shut the gate as the last cow made her way in. Laughing, he slapped Hannah's back, "Way to go! You rounded up the herd single-handedly!"

Hannah replied coyly, "Don't thank me. Those cattle herded your sister this time!"

STORY QUESTIONS

1. What is the main idea of paragraph two?
   a. It provides the problem in the story.
   b. It provides the solution to the story.
   c. It is the climax of the story.
   d. It provides the background and the setting of the story.

2. What is the meaning of the word *billowed* as used in the passage?
   a. rushed
   b. reverberated
   c. swirled
   d. descended

3. Which of the following did not happen in the story?
   a. Hannah was able to outsmart the cattle this year.
   b. Henry was thrilled with the fact the cattle went into the corral.
   c. Hannah's grandfather fought in the Mexican-American War.
   d. Hannah and Henry were herding cattle together.

Name _____   Date _____

MYREEL'S MOMENT

Myreel was just 13 years old when she entered the town's poetry contest. This contest usually attracted more established poets with many years of schooling under their belts, but Myreel's spirited personality had gotten her into situations like this before. Her confidence was enough to support her in moments of doubt.

"You're crazy," Jed had said. He had grown up as Myreel's neighbor since birth. Jed liked to put Myreel in her place. One time he had even put a skunk inside her carriage to get a rise out of her. Myreel sought revenge by putting a porcupine in Jed's bed. Myreel had done more things than most girls her age just because she was willing to try.

On the day of the poetry contest, Myreel selected a light blue dress with lace to wear. She blew a kiss to herself in the mirror.

Myreel sat nervously with the other poets, waiting for her name to be called. When it was her turn, Myreel rose to her feet. She read her poem in the most dramatic of voices. The crowd was moved and clapped enthusiastically.

It was no surprise at the end of the day when Myreel was presented the winner's trophy. Myreel saw Jed slink out the back after the award show. Myreel ran to catch up.

"So, Jed, am I still crazy?" asked Myreel.

"Crazy and amazing," said Jed, and he walked away shaking his head.

STORY QUESTIONS

1. Which sentence contains evidence that the story takes place in the past?
    a. Myreel was just 13 years old when she entered the town's poetry contest.
    b. Myreel selected to wear a light blue dress with lace.
    c. Myreel sat nervously with the other poets, waiting for her name to be called.
    d. One time he had even put a skunk inside her carriage to get a rise out of her.

2. Which paragraph explains the relationship between Myreel and Jed?
    a. first paragraph
    b. fourth paragraph
    c. second paragraph
    d. third paragraph

3. What is the meaning of the word *spirited* as used in the story?
    a. content and happy
    b. feisty and energetic
    c. ghostly and ghastly
    d. foreboding and sad

OPENING UP

Elizabeth blew out the candle and headed up the stairs for bed. It had been a long day, and she was tired. She climbed into the bed with her two little sisters. Elizabeth was the second-oldest in her family. She and her older brother Ben used to laugh and run and play as kids, but when their parents both died of the flu, they had assumed heavy loads of responsibility. Elizabeth's family wasn't the only one that had suffered losses from the flu epidemic. Many families in town had lost members of their family. Elizabeth's friend, Anne, had lost her mother, as well. Anne and Elizabeth got together frequently to can jams and vegetables.

Early the next morning, Elizabeth glanced out the window and saw Anne's wagon coming up the drive.

"That's odd," thought Elizabeth. "We didn't have any plans today."

Anne climbed out of the wagon and began pulling at a huge trunk. Ben stepped around Elizabeth to give Anne a hand.

"What's inside?" questioned Elizabeth.

"Dresses! More dresses than you will ever want," explained Anne. She opened the trunk to display beautiful dresses with lace and bows.

"No, I can't," said Elizabeth.

"Yes, you can," said Anne. "Mrs. Langston insisted that I take this trunk and share it with you. She said we could have every one of these dresses."

Elizabeth was stunned and didn't know what to say. "What can I say?"

"Say thank you," suggested Ben, giving Elizabeth a hug. "You deserve it."

STORY QUESTIONS

1. Which statement from the story would give a clue as to when the story took place?
   a. Elizabeth's family wasn't the only one that had suffered losses from the flu epidemic.
   b. She opened the trunk to display beautiful dresses with lace and bows.
   c. Anne and Elizabeth got together frequently to can jams and vegetables.
   d. She climbed into the bed with her two little sisters.

2. What is the meaning of the word *epidemic* as used in the story?
   a. plague
   b. monument
   c. orchestration
   d. eventt

3. Which of the following statements contains information from the story?
   a. Arrangements were being made for the children to be adopted.
   b. Anne had six brothers and sisters to care for.
   c. Elizabeth had learned to can from her mother.
   d. Elizabeth and Ben were orphans.

THE BULL RIDE

Jess jumped into the saddle and kicked his spurs in deep. He had to hurry to catch up. Every year, Jess's family had a rodeo. It was a family affair, and all of Jess's aunts, uncles, and cousins would be there.

Jess had been practicing all year for the bull-riding event. The family owned the meanest bull around. His name was Charley. Taking a ride on Charley was like asking to die.

Jess practiced on cows and steers. Ms. Bailey, Jess's teacher, had encouraged him to write about his experiences. Jess shared one story with the class. Billy Letcump laughed so hard that he fell off his chair when he heard the story. Jess got so mad that he walked over and broke his slate over Billy's head. Ms. Bailey liked the story, but she didn't like Jess's behavior. He was suspended from school for two days.

Thoughts of school vanished from Jess's mind as he slowed to a stop. When he reached the edge of the corral, he got off his horse and joined his clamoring cousins. Finally, it was his turn.

Uncle Pete helped Jess, while his dad kept Charley in control. The gate flew open before Jess had a minute to catch his breath.

Jess came to and could hear everyone screaming. What had happened?

"You won!" they all screamed. "You beat Uncle Quinn! You stayed on for four seconds!"

Jess rolled over and clutched his aching side—but not without grinning from ear to ear.

STORY QUESTIONS

1. What is meant by the word *clamoring* as used in the passage?
   a. whispering
   b. jumping
   c. crying
   d. bellowing

2. What can you conclude about Jess's bull ride?
   a. He was seriously injured.
   b. He was the new record-holder in the family for riding the bull.
   c. He was given a second chance.
   d. He was surprised to see he was riding Charley.

3. Which sentence helps you answer the previous question?
   a. Thoughts of school vanished from Jess's mind as he slowed to a stop.
   b. Jess rolled over and clutched his aching side, but not without grinning from ear to ear.
   c. "You beat Uncle Quinn! You stayed on for four seconds!"
   d. The gate flew open before Jess had a minute to catch his breath.

FIRST AID FRIENDSHIP

Esther jumped down out of the tree and straightened her clothes. She had climbed the tree to avoid being seen by her neighbor. Jimmy drove Esther crazy. He teased her incessantly, and just yesterday had dipped her braids in the ink at school. Her tips were still dyed black.

Esther walked through town. She made it to the general store and slipped inside. As she entered the store, she noticed a commotion going on in the corner. Esther wondered what was happening.

"He fainted and hit his head on the sink," yelled a girl as she pushed past Esther. "Get the doctor right away!"

"Who?" asked Esther, but nobody listened to her. Esther was scared of blood, but curiosity had gotten to her. She gasped and covered her mouth when she saw that it was Jimmy.

The crowd had thinned at this point, as people were looking for the doctor. Jimmy's eyes were closed and his head limp. Esther went up to Jimmy and put her apron on his forehead. Blood was everywhere.

"You've gotten yourself into a fine mess," said Esther. "I hope you aren't going to die. All those things I've said about you . . . why I could . . ." Esther's voice faded.

"You could what?" asked Jimmy. Had he been listening to her the whole time? Esther almost dropped Jimmy's head at this point.

Instead, she gathered her wits and said, "Jimmy Stevens, I could just spit!" Jimmy chuckled and closed his eyes.

STORY QUESTIONS

1. What is the main idea of the first paragraph?
   a. to explain the meaning of the word *incessantly*
   b. to explain the relationship between Esther and Jimmy
   c. to provide background as to Esther's first aid training
   d. to explain why Esther's hair is black

2. What would be a good title for this story?
   a. "First Aid Guidelines"
   b. "New-found Friendship"
   c. "Help from a Neighbor"
   d. "Getting Needled"

3. What is another word for *incessantly* as used in this story?
   a. instructional
   b. purposeful
   c. questioning
   d. non-stop

116

I AM JAPANESE

Lin's family had been at this internment camp for three months now. Since the bombing of Pearl Harbor, the American government didn't feel it could trust the Japanese Americans and placed them in camps situated in the desert.

Lin and his family slept in barracks with lots of other people. Sleeping conditions were poor, and it was noisy. Dust storms raced through the camps, and swirling clouds of dust were everywhere.

One evening Dad asked Lin, "What's wrong?" He could tell that something wasn't quite right.

"I just don't get why we're here. I don't understand why there's a guard up there. I don't get why we live in a prison."

"It's not a prison: it's a camp," interrupted Dad.

"What's the difference? We couldn't leave if we wanted to. That's a prison, Dad," replied Lin.

That's when Lin's father decided to make a baseball field. This would keep people's minds off their troubles. Night and day they dug up the sagebrush and cleared a field.

Weeks later, Lin circled the baseball field for the second time that day. He was hoping to get three home runs for the evening. He glanced up at the guard on the tower. As usual, the guard kept his gun ready and poised.

Lin's dad waved him in safely. "Way to go, Lin! That was an awesome home run!" yelled his dad.

"Thanks, Dad," replied Lin. He hustled back to the bench. He was sure he had another one in him.

STORY QUESTIONS

1. Using the context clues, what is the meaning of the word *internment* as used in the passage?
   a. imprisonment
   b. realignment
   c. cultural
   d. problematic

2. According to the passage, which sentence shows how Lin feels about living in the internment camp?
   a. He glanced up at the guard on the tower.
   b. "I don't get why we live in a prison."
   c. As usual, the guard kept his gun ready and poised.
   d. He hustled back to the bench.

3. What is the purpose of the first paragraph?
   a. to introduce the characters in the story
   b. to explain the problem and resolution in the story
   c. to provide the background and the setting of the story
   d. none of the above

DAILY Warm-Up 14   Name _____   Date _____

BLISSFUL GRATITUDE

The Jensens were picking apples off the tree. They wanted to get as many as they could.

"This one's gross," yelled young Billy. "It has worms in it." Billy threw it across the yard. Mother scurried to pick up the apple.

"Now Billy, it may seem gross, but we can cut the worm out. We can't afford to waste anything."

"Why not?" asked Sue.

Mother calmly explained, "Sue, things are getting worse. You know how we've been trying to save as much money as we can on this farm. Farm prices have dropped again. Daddy's having a hard time making payments on the farm."

"I miss the days when we weren't worried and grouchy all the time," said Sue. "I miss the days when we were a happy family."

Just then, a car drove into the driveway of the farm. From a distance, mother and the children watched a man put a box on their doorstep."

"What's that, Mommy?" asked Billy.

"I bet it's another bill needing to be paid," she sighed.

"Tell that man that we don't want any," stammered Sue angrily. Growing up in the Depression was tough.

"Can I go see what it is?" asked Billy.

"Yes," said Mother.

Billy ran across the yard and peered in the box. "It's a box of food!" he hollered. Mother smiled and said, "Well, that was so nice. I guess there's no room for worry or grouchiness today!" Sue smiled and ran across the yard to take a look.

STORY QUESTIONS

1. Which sentence shows the time period in which the story was written?
   a. Sue smiled and ran across the yard to take a look.
   b. "I miss the days when we weren't worried and grouchy all the time."
   c. "We can't afford to waste anything."
   d. Growing up in the Depression was tough.

2. What conclusions can be drawn about how Sue feels about the Depression?
   a. She doesn't know very much about it.
   b. Sue is learning about the Depression from a book she's reading.
   c. She is tired of the affects it is having on her family.
   d. Sue thinks it has important lessons to be learned.

3. After reading the passage, which of the following helps you answer the previous question?
   a. Sue smiled and ran across the yard to take a look.
   b. "I miss the days when we weren't worried and grouchy all the time," said Sue.
   c. "Tell that man that we don't want any," stammered Sue angrily.
   d. "Daddy's having a hard time making payments on the farm."

CURIOUS JOE

Joe hurried home after school. He had plans to go to Miss Annie's house. Rumor was that Miss Annie had died three weeks ago, and no one had discovered her body yet. Joe wanted to check it out. This was the most excitement Joe had ever experienced. Growing up in a small town in 1950s was definitely not the height of adventure.

After a snack, Joe grabbed his binoculars and headed for the back pasture. He figured he'd get to Miss Annie's house through the fields so that no one from the street would see him walking up to her house.

As he stopped at the field just outside Miss Annie's back door, he stopped to catch his breath. His heart was racing. What if he found Miss Annie's body?

Slowly he opened the back door. It creaked as it went. He stepped inside and glanced around, but he didn't see anything unusual. He sniffed the air, but it smelled normal. Joe began climbing the stairs. When he reached the top of the stairs, a door opened and a figure came running at Joe with a bat! Whack!

"Get out of my house, you intruder!"

"What?" Joe asked and then opened his eyes. He stared into the face of Miss Annie. He didn't say another word, but jumped up and ran out the door as quickly as he could. He didn't stop running until he got to his house. He decided then and there that his spying days were over!

STORY QUESTIONS

1. Using the context clues, what does the word *height* mean as used in this passage?
   a. pinnacle or top
   b. intensify or interrogate
   c. gather or collect
   d. chide or scold

2. According to the passage, what did Joe neglect to do when making his plans?
   a. He didn't talk to anybody about his plans.
   b. He forgot his plan at home.
   c. He lost his way and ended up in the wrong house.
   d. He went at the wrong time of day.

3. What is the theme of this story?
   a. If at first you don't succeed, try again.
   b. If you try hard enough, you can win.
   c. It's important to knock out your competition.
   d. Mind your own business.

SKY HIGH

Jeff and Chris breathed heavily as they climbed the mountain. The switchbacks were getting steeper and steeper. The boys had slowed considerably since they had started. Chris could tell that Jeff was losing steam.

"Do you want to sit for a minute?" asked Chris.

"Yeah," replied Jeff in a hollow voice.

The boys sat down on pine needles and took swigs of water in an attempt to cool off.

"We are at the same point where we quit last time," commented Jeff.

"That's right," said Chris, "so we should keep going to get further up this mountain."

"I just don't think I have it in me today," said Jeff.

"C'mon Jeff, you've got to try," encouraged Chris.

Jeff thought about it and then decided he did want to give it a try. Before he could change his mind, he bolted up the hill. He climbed so fast he almost fell over.

"Dude! Slow down," called Chris.

"No way. If I stop, I'm never going to make it," yelled Jeff. He continued his push up the mountain. Chris followed close behind. Each grueling step shot pain throughout their bodies, but they just kept going. Higher and higher they climbed. Before long, they found themselves just below the top of the mountain. Jeff looked back at Chris.

"Are you ready?" asked Jeff.

"More than I'll ever be," answered Chris.

The two climbed to the top of the mountain and watched the sun rising. It was a beautiful morning.

STORY QUESTIONS

1. Using the context clues, what does the word *hollow* mean?
   a. filled   c. vacant
   b. perplexed   d. ferocious

2. According to the passage, what helped Jeff make it up the mountain?
   a. He was in better shape than Chris.
   b. He was motivated by a stronger incentive than Chris.
   c. He knew his friends were waiting at the top.
   d. He didn't want to fail again.

3. What is the main idea of the passage?
   a. Being creative and using many resources can help you accomplish a task.
   b. If you try hard enough, you can do it.
   c. It's important to knock out your competition.
   d. Having a good friend can be helpful at times.

DAILY Warm-Up 2   Name _____   Date _____

NOT INVITED

Soon after Sandy got to school, Erica showed up. Sandy noticed Erica shove a bag in her desk. She wondered what it was. Later in the morning, Sandy saw Erica slip something to Jill under the desk. When she saw Erica slip something to Beth at lunch, she couldn't resist.

"What are you doing, Erica? Are you having a party without me?" demanded Sandy.

"Oh, Sandy, it's nothing," said Erica.

"What kind of friend has a party and doesn't invite her best friend?" thought Sandy. She knew her birthday wasn't coming for another six months.

Sandy sat on the bus with another girl and made sure there wasn't room for Erica. Erica sat with someone else, and Sandy noticed that she gave this girl an envelope, too.

"The nerve!" thought Sandy.

That night after dinner, there was a knock on the door. Sandy was surprised to see Jill from next door. She invited Sandy to go with her to Erica's party.

"I'm not going," explained Sandy. "We just aren't friends anymore."

"Oh, you have to go," said Jill, and she took Sandy's arm.

Imagine Sandy's surprise when the door opened at Erica's house and everyone screamed, "Surprise!"

"What? It's not my birthday," said Sandy.

"That's right. This is a half-birthday party. If I did it on your birthday, then it wouldn't be a surprise," said Erica, and she gave Sandy a hug.

STORY QUESTIONS

1. Which sentence shows how Sandy felt about Erica?
   a. "What kind of friend has a party and doesn't invite her best friend?"
   b. "What? It's not my birthday."
   c. "I'm not going."
   d. "What are you doing, Erica?"

2. The first paragraph shares with the reader . . .
   a. how to solve the problem.
   b. what the problem was.
   c. the disagreements between the children.
   d. the relationship between the children.

3. What is the main idea of the passage?
   a. Being creative and using many resources can help you accomplish a task.
   b. If you try hard enough, you can do it.
   c. It's important to knock out your competition.
   d. Don't jump to conclusions.

SNOW BUNNY

Kristi rode up the mountain with a group of friends from school. All of the kids in the car knew how to ski except for Kristi. This was her first trip, and she was nervous.

"You're going to do fine," said Lindsey, Kristi's friend.

The night before, Kristi had read a book about skiing. She learned how to stand, and she learned about the snow plow. She was excited to try, but she was so worried about falling—or even worse, crashing into someone.

Lindsey explained that the bunny hill had a towrope that would pull you up the short hill. Kristi made it to the top of the bunny hill and put her legs into snow-plow position. Kristi gathered speed faster and faster. She could see the line of beginning skiers just below her.

"Help!" she hollered. Lindsey raced down to help Kristi, but it was too late.

Crash! Kristi plowed into the line of skiers and took them down one at a time. No one was seriously hurt, just a little shaken. Kristi was the most shaken of all and kept saying, "I'm so sorry!"

By the time Lindsey caught up, she got the giggles. "Wow, Kristi, I think we need to work on your snow plow."

"Snow plow? I think I had my snow plow down just fine," said Kristi. Lindsey started giggling again.

"What I need is for you to help me with my snow *stop*!" said Kristi.

STORY QUESTIONS

1. Which paragraph explains what Kristi did the night before?
   a. first paragraph
   b. last paragraph
   c. third paragraph
   d. second paragraph

2. What inferences can you make about how Kristi will ski the second time down?
   a. She is going to go much faster.
   b. She is going to forget the bunny hill and go for the regular hills.
   c. She is going to be yelling and screaming at Lindsey when she does it.
   d. She is going to go much slower this time.

3. What does Kristi need to learn about skiing?
   a. She's lucky to have a dad willing to let her try.
   b. Reading a book about skiing doesn't fully teach you how to ski.
   c. She needs better friends to help her.
   d. She needs to give up on the idea.

DAILY Warm-Up 4 Name _____ Date _____

ACHOO!

"The recipe calls for two tablespoons of pepper," said Dillon.

"Are you sure that's right?" asked Miranda. "That seems like a lot!"

"Yep, it's right. Remember, this isn't just any soup: this is special soup to help mom feel better."

Miranda dumped the two tablespoons of pepper in and stirred the broth. The onions came next, and then the carrots.

Miranda sniffed the soup and began sneezing. "Whew! That's a lot of pepper."

"It's going to be great," assured Dillon.

The soup simmered for 15 minutes. Dillon grabbed a soup bowl and began ladling the soup.

"This is going to be so good for Mom's cold," said Miranda.

Dillon dropped a cloth over his arm and Miranda got out a tray.

"Here we come, Mom," called Dillon.

"Achoo!" said Mom. "What's this?"

"It's homemade soup, just for you. It's going to work better than medicine."

Mom took a big sniff of the soup in her lap and immediately started sneezing. She couldn't stop.

"Taste it, Mom," encouraged Dillon.

"She can't. It has too much pepper!" protested Miranda.

"It's okay," interrupted Mom. "It's clearing my sinuses. I can finally breathe again! How much pepper is in there?"

"Two tablespoons," said Dillon.

"The recipe calls for two TEASPOONS!" shouted Miranda.

"This is the best," said Mom. "Bring that soup back here again! Achoo!"

STORY QUESTIONS

1. Which of the following statements is <u>not</u> true?
   a. Miranda told Dillon to add two tablespoons of pepper.
   b. Mom was a good sport and made her kids feel good about helping her.
   c. Miranda was frustrated that Dillon put too much pepper in the soup.
   d. Miranda trusted Dillon's instructions at the beginning of the passage.

2. What conclusions can be drawn about Miranda and Dillon's mom?
   a. She is an emotional person and cries a lot.
   b. She is supportive and understanding.
   c. She will probably never eat soup again.
   d. She tries to take over every situation.

3. After reading the passage, which of the following helps you answer the previous question?
   a. "How much pepper is in there?"
   b. "It's okay," interrupted Mom. "It's clearing my sinuses."
   c. Mom took a big sniff of the soup in her lap.
   d. She couldn't stop sneezing.

DAILY
Warm-Up 5

Name _____ Date _____

MATH WHIZ

"I've had it!" screamed Rebecca. "I am so tired of math; I hope I never see it again in my life."

"That sounds pretty dramatic, doesn't it?" asked Dad.

"Dad, I'm serious! I just don't get it."

"It will come but you have to keep working on it. Now, let's look over the last problem," said Dad.

"Ugh! I just can't stand this subject," said Rebecca as her dad perused her work.

"Rebecca, you are doing fine," Dad said calmly. "Now show me how you worked this problem." Rebecca couldn't stand the thought of reviewing her math. She thought her stomach would turn. Her brain always seemed to look at math problems wrong. When she was right, she thought she was wrong. It was a no-win situation.

In fourth grade, Rebecca had been asked to take a math test to see where she was academically. Rebecca would have rather died. She barely made it through the test before she started crying.

"Alright, Dad. I took this number and doubled it. Then I subtracted it by three and got fifty-seven. With that number, I divided it into two," Rebecca said defiantly.

"Well, if you did that . . ." started Dad.

"That's it!" Rebecca threw her math book on the floor and her papers into the air.

"Let me finish. . . ." interrupted Dad. "If you did that, then you got it right!"

Rebecca was speechless. "You've got to be kidding me." Dad shook his head and walked out of the room laughing.

STORY QUESTIONS

1. Which statement best describes Rebecca based on the reading passage?
   a. Rebecca is lazy and tired most of the time.
   b. Rebecca is curious and likes to explore.
   c. Rebecca is timid, shy, and introverted.
   d. Rebecca is impatient and gets frustrated easily.

2. Which sentence explains the problem in this story?
   a. Rebecca couldn't stand the thought of reviewing her math.
   b. When she was right, she thought she was wrong.
   c. Rebecca was speechless.
   d. In fourth grade, Rebecca had been asked to take a math test to see where she was academically.

3. What does the word *perused* mean as used in the passage?
   a. indicated   c. restricted
   b. looked over carefully   d. flippantly

DAILY NEWS

Pat climbed up on his bike and lifted the heavy bag of newspapers over his shoulder. It was another day. He was in his usual spot at 5:00 A.M., delivering newspapers. Pat had been doing the job for two years and recounted his crazy memories of early hours and dogs.

Pat opted to start on the second street to avoid the bulldog on First Street. As Pat pulled up alongside the first house, he threw the paper. It landed directly on the door step. Just then, directly in front of him in the street was Max, the bulldog.

"What?" called Pat, screeching to a halt. "What is he doing here?"

Max began growling, and Pat began thinking of his options. He could just start screaming, but no one would hear him. Pat hopped on the bike again and pedaled as fast as he could. As soon as he passed Max, the dog began chasing him. Pat swerved into an alley and turned to see if Max was following.

Before he knew what happened Pat was sailing through the air. He landed with a slump. He awoke to Max growling at him. He got up, grabbed his crumpled bike, and headed for home.

That morning Mom asked, "How was your route? Did you run into any dogs?"

"No, Mom. I got in a fight with a garbage can."

"What?" questioned Mom.

"Let's just leave it at that. It sounds better that way," said Pat chuckling.

STORY QUESTIONS

1. Which of the following statements is true?
   a. Pat is just beginning his job with the newspaper.
   b. Pat really likes the bulldog on First Street.
   c. Pat uses a strategy to avoid Max.
   d. Pat runs into a trash can trying to get out of delivering papers.

2. What is the meaning of the word *recounted* used in the story?
   a. directions
   b. ignored
   c. exaggerated
   d. reviewed

3. Which word best describes Pat's reaction to his experience?
   a. patient
   b. annoyed
   c. insistent
   d. resilient

DAILY
Warm-Up 7

Name _____

Date _____

YOU LIVE IN A ZOO

"Kevin?" called Mom. "Did you feed the monkeys yet?"

"Working on it," replied Kevin. Kevin and his family lived in a zoo. It seemed a strange place to live except that Kevin's parents were both zoo keepers and scientists. They had been studying animals for years.

On this particular morning, Kevin was anxious to get his feeding chores done and go skateboarding with his friends. Feeding the animals was a daily responsibility.

"Done!" hollered Kevin. "I'm going to go now, okay?"

"Wait," called Kevin's mom. "I only count six chimpanzees. What happened to Arthur?"

Kevin walked into the cage from the back. He didn't believe his mom. But sure enough, he could only count six chimpanzees. This usually meant that they were hiding in a tree somewhere, but it still caused panic for Mom. Kevin began searching with his mother.

Where could that chimp have gone? Arthur had done this before. He was a curious chimp and was always getting into trouble. Kevin's mom was really panicking this time. They couldn't see or hear Arthur anywhere.

"Kevin, I think he's really gone this time," called Mom.

"No, Mom, he's not," said Kevin calmly.

"How can you tell?" asked Mom.

"Because I can see him in the tree right behind you. He's crouched low so you can't see him," explained Kevin, smiling.

"That rascal!" called Mom.

"He's just playing hide-and-seek, Mom. It's all in a day's work for a chimpanzee!" said Kevin.

STORY QUESTIONS

1. What would be a good title for this story?
   a. "Lost and Found Chimpanzee"   c. "Boy Meets Ape"
   b. "Family Matters"   d. "Process of Learning"

2. What can you conclude about Kevin after reading the passage?
   a. He is loved and adored by the monkeys.   c. He is learning to skate board.
   b. He is a good at math.   d. He is helpful and calm.

3. Which sentence helps you answer the previous question?
   a. Kevin began searching with his mother.
   b. Kevin walked into the cage from the back.
   c. Kevin and his family lived in a zoo.
   d. Kevin was anxious to get his feeding chores done and go skateboarding with his friends.

THE DIVE

Jonathan stretched his muscles. Each year, Jonathan and his friends participated in the diving contest at the community pool. Divers from all over the county came to participate.

The competition began with all the divers making an assigned dive. They were given points based on how they pointed their toes, tucked their heads, and on the form of the dive. Jonathan performed his dive and scraped up enough points to move on to the next round.

At this level, the diver could select the dive of his or her choice. Thoughts of the final dive came into Jonathan's mind. All the divers gathered around discussing who was left to compete. Jonathan noticed a poor boy that had on an old swimsuit. Jonathan laughed with his peers about how this boy managed to slip into this level of divers.

The boy was first, and he made his way up to the highest board. He made his dive and then sat down. It was a sloppy dive without much finesse. Jonathan was next. He performed his dive without a hitch.

All the divers were stunned when the poor boy's name was announced. The judge threw up his hands and said, "His dive may not have been the cleanest, but it was the riskiest by far. I gave points for guts and for trying." Jonathan walked away shaking his head, determined to do it differently next year.

STORY QUESTIONS

1. Which of the following statements is true?
   a. The diver was given special treatment by the judges.
   b. Not all of the divers in the competition considered all the aspects of selecting their dives.
   c. Jonathan didn't spend enough time practicing his dive.
   d. Jonathan was nervous after he saw the boy's dive.

2. What would be a good title for this story?
   a. "The Divers"
   b. "The Difficulty of the Dive"
   c. "Diving Concerns"
   d. "Process of Elimination"

3. What is another word for *peers* as used in this story?
   a. instructors
   b. judges
   c. relatives
   d. competitors

GIRLS JUST WANT TO HAVE FUN

The alarm went off as usual at 6:00 in the morning. Jessica rolled over, turned it off, and let out a groan. She met up with her dancing team, and they loaded the bus.

Jessica's friend Aja plopped down beside her in the seat and put her head on a pillow. "It's so early in the morning!" complained Aja. "I only got, like, an hour of sleep!"

"You'll live," said Jessica. "This is going to be an awesome day. You could've stayed up all night and it would still be awesome!"

As the bus pulled into the stadium, Jessica felt her heart jump. The girls began stretching and preparing for their first dance. When it was time, their team strolled with big smiles onto the stage. The team was hyped and ready to go. Just then, the cue was given and the music started. The girls began the dance they had practiced a hundred times.

All of a sudden, the music stopped. A gasp came from the audience. But the team pretended like nothing happened and kept going. They didn't miss a beat. It was amazing for Jessica to see her teammates in her peripheral vision. When the finale came, the audience jumped to their feet clapping their hands.

It was no surprise that afternoon when their team was awarded the first-place trophy.

As Jessica sat down in the bus for the long ride home, she smiled to herself and thought, "All in a day's work! Girls just want to have fun."

STORY QUESTIONS

1. The main idea of the first paragraph is to . . .
   a. set the tone of the story.
   b. introduce some of the characters.
   c. introduce foreshadowing.
   d. explain the climax of the story.

2. Another word for *peripheral* is . . .
   a. blinding.
   b. formation.
   c. side.
   d. secondary.

3. Which sentence explains the problem in this story?
   a. The music went off during their performance.
   b. Jessica and Aja had to get up very early in the morning.
   c. Aja is not a morning person.
   d. Jessica's team made a mistake in the competition but came back to win.

STIFF STRANGER

Jenna had been planning a sleepover for as long as she could remember. She had made all the arrangements. She had cleaned up the basement so that there would be plenty of room to spread out and have sleeping bags. She had invited six friends over, ordered pizza, and picked up three scary movies.

By seven o'clock, all the girls had arrived and they had downed the first pizza. Jenna happened to glance up at the window. She screamed when she saw a man standing in the yard. All the girls screamed and asked what was wrong. Jenna pointed to the window, and all the girls screamed when they saw the man.

The girls crept up to the window again to get a good look at him. They needed a plan. Jenna's parents had gone to the store. Jenna went to get a baseball bat from her brother's room. Then Mandy asked, "Are you really going to use that?"

"I don't know, but it makes me feel safer," explained Jenna.

"What do you think he wants?" asked Brooke.

"I don't know, but I'm not going to talk to him," said Jenna.

"He's just standing there not moving at all," commented Mandy.

"Wait a minute," said Samantha. "That's not a man: that's a scarecrow."

"Whew! You're right," replied Jenna. "Let's go watch another show. I want to get scared some more!" Jenna shook her head, smiled, and put the bat back in her brother's room.

STORY QUESTIONS

1. What would be a good title for this story?
   a. "Lost and Found at Night"
   b. "Stiff Competition"
   c. "Scared by a Man"
   d. "A Real Scare"

2. What can you conclude about Jenna after reading the passage?
   a. She is loved and adored by her friends.
   b. She is a good at math.
   c. She is learning self-defense.
   d. She is easily scared.

3. Which sentence helps you answer the previous question?
   a. By seven o'clock, all the girls had arrived and they had downed the first pizza.
   b. Jenna happened to glance up at the window.
   c. She screamed when she saw a man standing in the yard.
   d. Jenna shook her head and smiled and put the bat back in her brother's room.

A LITTLE MOTIVATION

Brennan stretched before his last cross-country race of the year. The season had been long, and he was glad it was almost over. In fact, Brennan didn't ever want to race again. He was tired. Brennan had raced in every 5K and 10K around. The excitement was wearing thin.

"Way to go!" called Coach Thompson. He was always encouraging Brennan. In fact, Coach Thompson was a big reason Brennan had stayed on the team. He didn't want to let Coach Thompson down.

Brennan finished the last lap of the course and headed out for the cross-country portion of the race. The race went over the hills and dunes of the desert. It wasn't unusual to spot desert animals scurrying by. Brennan was a little melancholy when he ran. The runners ahead of him were in front by a good distance. He would really have to push himself if he wanted a medal.

Just then, Brennan looked down and saw a rattlesnake in the path ahead of him. It was coiled and hissing.

"Yikes!" yelled Brennan, and he jumped in the air over the snake. Brennan took off in a sprint like he never had before. Brennan kept running until he got past the leader. Racing down to the finish line, he could hardly believe it.

"Nice finish!" hollered his coach. "How did you manage that? I didn't know you had it in you!"

"Just a little motivation," said Brennan with a twinkle in his eye. Racing suddenly felt good again.

STORY QUESTIONS

1. What is meant by the phrase *wearing thin* as used in the story?
   a. very unorganized
   b. shabby looking
   c. historically incorrect
   d. getting mundane

2. What do you think Brennan's plans will be concerning cross country next year?
   a. He will quit because he is tired.
   b. He will have to talk to Coach Thompson about it.
   c. He will probably run cross country again the next year.
   d. He is unsure and uncertain.

3. Which sentence from the story will help you predict Brennan's plans?
   a. Racing suddenly felt good again.
   b. Brennan was a little melancholy when he ran.
   c. In fact, Coach Thompson was a big reason Brennan had stayed on the team.
   d. He would really have to push himself if he wanted a medal.

THE GOLDFISH GULP

The sun was starting to set on the horizon as Peter went in to change for the beach party at the club. He was excited to meet some of the other kids that would be spending their summer on the island. He was still very uncomfortable and felt so new.

As Peter and his parents went out onto the patio where the music was playing, he felt a knot in his stomach again. He was so nervous. What if the kids thought he was dumb? He looked over to see the group of boys coming over to his table.

"Hey, Peter," called Zack.

"Hey," answered Peter.

"Come sit with us," motioned Zack.

Peter joined the group and started laughing and joking with the rest of them. All of sudden, Zack grabbed a goldfish that was swimming in a bowl on the table. He threw his head back and gulped down the goldfish. Peter was stunned.

"Your turn," said Zack, motioning to Peter.

Peter looked at the goldfish and replied, "I'm just not much of a fisherman. Thanks, anyway." The boys laughed at Peter's joke.

"Whew!" thought Peter. "I survived that one." But did he want to survive any more? Peter realized that he didn't want to be a part of this group after all, and slowly meandered back to where his parents were sitting, back where the only fish being eaten were on the dinner plates. For the first time that summer, Peter finally felt at home.

STORY QUESTIONS

1. What does the word *meandered* mean?
   a. crisscrossed   c. strolled
   b. aware of   d. awakened

2. How was Peter able to avoid eating the goldfish?
   a. He was able to explain why it's not a good idea to eat a goldfish.
   b. He made it look like a dumb idea.
   c. He managed to get the group to consider eating different fish.
   d. He made a joke.

3. Which sentence helps answer the question above?
   a. He threw his head back and gulped down the goldfish.
   b. Peter looked at the goldfish and replied, "I'm just not much of a fisherman. Thanks, anyway."
   c. Peter was stunned.
   d. He was still very uncomfortable and felt so new.

DAILY Warm-Up 13

Name _____ Date _____

SETH'S COURAGE

Seth was walking down the school hallway when he saw a group of boys huddled in a corner. The boys were laughing and joking around. He wondered what was so funny, so he walked up close to listen.

Sam, one of boys, noticed and said, "Seth, old buddy. What are you doing in social studies?"

Unsure what to say, Seth replied, "Listening to Mr. Oldham's lecture."

"No, I mean during the lesson," said Sam.

"I don't think I get what you mean," replied Seth.

"I dare you to put gum on Franklin's chair," whispered Sam.

"I'll think about it," responded Seth. He knew that if he didn't do what the group said, they would turn on him. On the other hand, Franklin was a kid who had mental disabilities. He seemed nice and was always smiling.

"How could I do that to Franklin?" wondered Seth.

Just then, the bell rang, and the boys filed into class. Sam slipped Seth a stick of gum. Seth knew he was supposed to chew it up and put it in Franklin's chair.

At that moment, Franklin entered the room with some commotion. Seth could hardly believe it when Franklin sat next to him. Sam kicked Seth's chair and started laughing.

Seth took the piece of gum and handed it to Franklin, "Franklin, would you like a piece of gum?" Seth turned back just in time to see Sam's scowl. He couldn't help smiling to himself.

STORY QUESTIONS

1. Which of the following statements would be new information to the reader?
   a. Franklin is nice to everybody.
   b. Seth is given a dare to put gum on Franklin's chair.
   c. Seth and Franklin are neighbors.
   d. Seth is trying hard to fit in with the new group of kids.

2. Which sentence explains the problem in this story?
   a. Sam knew that if he didn't do what the group said, they would turn on him.
   b. Seth knew he was supposed to put gum in Franklin's chair, but he didn't want to.
   c. Sam slipped Seth a stick of gum.
   d. Just then the bell rang and the boys filed into class.

3. What is the resolution to the story?
   a. Seth turned back just in time to see Sam's scowl.
   b. He couldn't help smiling to himself.
   c. Seth took the piece of gum and handed it to Franklin.
   d. Sam kicked Seth's chair and started laughing.

Name _____ Date _____

DANCE FEVER

Dance Fever was a group of neighborhood girls who loved to dance and put on performances. The girls practiced for hours on end. Finally, the day of the show arrived.

All the girls were afraid they would forget their parts. But that wasn't the problem at all. In fact, they were about to face their worst fear ever.

Lights, camera, action! It was time for the show. The girls put on their costumes and got ready backstage. The parents were assembling in the audience section of the basement. There was a slight glitch in the technical equipment, but that was soon remedied.

The first two dances went off without a hitch. The next dance required a pyramid by the girls. They had practiced this part over and over. The problem came when Ashlyn slipped on Lexi's knee. It was an innocent mistake that had drastic results. Ashlyn came tumbling down. Along with her went Lexi, Caitlyn, Anne, and Elise. It was a pile of arms and legs. Moans and groans were heard from the girls. A gasp rose from the audience.

With nothing left to do, the girls all rose to their feet and took a bow. This thrilled the audience, who were afraid of what might happen next. The audience jumped to their feet, giving the girls a standing ovation. In a most unexpected way, the girls had gotten the response they had dreamed of!

STORY QUESTIONS

1. Which paragraph explains the problem in the story?
   a. first paragraph
   b. last paragraph
   c. third paragraph
   d. fourth paragraph

2. What inferences can you make about the Dance Fever girls?
   a. They are strict with each other.
   b. They have very high expectations.
   c. They don't take themselves too seriously and can adjust easily.
   d. They are learning about peer pressure.

3. What is the meaning of the word *remedied* as used in the story?
   a. resolved
   b. quickly
   c. instrumental
   d. systematically

Name _____ Date _____

TEASPOON OR CUP?

Wren loved autumn. She loved baking cookies and sipping hot chocolate. People always complimented her on her cookies. On this particular Saturday, Wren had it in her mind to make molasses cookies. These were a family favorite, and Wren's mother had gotten the original recipe from her great-great-grandmother. Just thinking of the cookies made her mouth water.

When she measured the cinnamon and poured it in, she realized that she would not have enough cloves. She called to her mother upstairs, "Where are some more cloves? We are out."

"How could that be?" asked her mother. "I just bought more cloves the other day!"

"Well, I've used the rest of that bottle, and now it is empty," replied Wren.

"Wow!" said her mother, "Then get the extra bottle from the bottom of the cupboard."

It wasn't long before Wren was ready to pull out the first batch. Wren decided to reward herself with the first bite.

"Yuck!" exclaimed Wren. She spit the cookie into the sink.

"What happened?" asked her mother as she took a bite. She spit her cookie out, as well.

"I don't know," said Wren.

"How many cloves did you put in?" asked Mother.

"Just a half of a cup," responded Wren.

"Half of a cup?" asked Mother incredulously. "Half of a cup? It only calls for half of a teaspoon!"

"Oh!" replied Wren. "Did I tell you I made some bird cookies?" she quickly improvised. Mother chuckled and helped Wren set the cookies outside for the birds.

STORY QUESTIONS

1. Using inference, what were Wren's feelings about her cookies?
   a. indifferent   c. embarrassed
   b. upset   d. approves

2. Which sentence indicates Wren's feelings about the new batch of cookies?
   a. "Oh!" replied Wren. "Did I tell you I made some bird cookies?" she quickly improvised.
   b. Mother chuckled and helped Wren set the cookies outside for the birds.
   c. "Yuck!" exclaimed Wren. She spit the cookie into the sink.
   d. "How could that be?" asked her mother.

3. Which sentence is an example from the story that demonstrates Wren's baking abilities?
   a. She loved baking cookies and sipping hot chocolate.
   b. Just thinking of the cookies made her mouth water.
   c. Wren had it in her mind to make molasses cookies.
   d. People always complimented her on her cookies.

Fiction: Contemporary Realistic

Name _____ **Date** _____

MADE IN MEXICO

Rosario and his family had just moved to town. They had emigrated from Mexico, their home country, looking for better work. The Gonzalez family was "keyed up" for this chance, but they were surprised to find that this new country had different people, smells, habits, and behaviors.

The first thing that was new for Rosario was the clothes that the other kids in the neighborhood wore to school. They didn't wear jeans and T-shirts like Rosario was used to: they wore blue shirts and tan pants. Rosario's mom explained that he would have to wear the same clothes when he went to school. That wasn't a pleasant thought.

Rosario's neighbor, Kevin, invited Rosario to come play soccer at the park with the other kids. Kevin was trying to help Rosario feel welcome. Rosario wasn't excited about this. He wished he could play *futbol*, like he did back in Mexico. Imagine his surprise when he showed up and found kids running around kicking a soccer ball. *Futbol* and soccer were the same thing!

This was going to be great! Rosario headed off to the field in chase of the other boys. He caught up and joined in the kicking and dribbling. Kevin smiled as he saw Rosario attack the ball. It sailed through the air and landed in the net just behind the goalie's neck. Wow! The boys stood in disbelief.

Kevin started clapping. He called out, *"Tu es mi amigo!"*

Rosario called back, "You are my friend, too." The United States wasn't so bad, after all.

STORY QUESTIONS

1. Which statement best explains the first thing Kevin did to make Rosario feel welcome?
    a. He called out, *"Tu es mi amigo!"*
    b. Kevin invited Rosario to come play soccer at the park with the other kids.
    c. Kevin started clapping.
    d. Kevin smiled as he saw Rosario attack the ball.

2. Which sentence explains the problem in the story?
    a. Kevin was rude to Rosario.
    b. The other kids playing soccer were rude to Rosario.
    c. Rosario was new and felt uncomfortable.
    d. Rosario wanted to move back to Mexico.

3. What is the meaning of the words *keyed up* in the story?
    a. unbiased and disinterested
    b. secretive and confidential
    c. excited and thrilled
    d. none of the above

WASHED ASHORE

Melinda and her brother Ben were climbing the rocks on the beach one day when they happened to come across a bone. A bone may not seem that unusual, but this was a big bone. It wasn't one you'd usually find lying on the beach.

"I wonder why this is here," Melinda thought aloud. "Why would there be a big bone like this lying around? It looks like a human bone."

"That sounds creepy," said Ben.

Just then, a truck drove up to the beach. Melinda watched a man get out with his dog. The two began running up and down the beach looking for something.

"Alright," said Ben. "Let's figure out where this bone came from."

The two began combing the beach looking for other bone pieces. Melinda was scared and worried. Ben didn't say much. They pondered on the bone's origin.

Just then, the dog came running up to Ben, who was carrying the bone. The dog began barking.

"Oh, there it is," said the man.

"Where is what?" asked Ben.

"That's Franklin's bone. We've been looking for it. We left it here yesterday."

"And just where did you get the bone?" asked Melinda skeptically.

The man started laughing when he realized what the kids must be thinking. "This is a deer bone. We brought it here to the beach," explained the man. "Case closed?" he asked.

"Case closed," said Ben as a little smile crept onto his face. Melinda just shook her head.

STORY QUESTIONS

1. Which word best describes how Melinda and Ben felt at the end of the story?
   a. organized
   b. relieved
   c. annoyed
   d. exhausted

2. Which paragraph helps you answer the previous question?
   a. last paragraph
   b. first paragraph
   c. fourth paragraph
   d. third paragraph

3. Another good title for the passage could be . . .
   a. "A Bony Beach."
   b. "Melinda and Ben."
   c. "Give Me My Bone."
   d. "The Mystery Bone."

THE ENCOUNTER

It was very cold outside, and Jeff was freezing. He had on a bunch of blankets, but he could still see his breath in the air. Jeff and his family had come up the mountain for a weekend of skiing and snowmobiling.

Jeffrey knew the fire needed more fuel. He could hear his dad snoring, so he knew that he was fast asleep. He put on his slippers and coat. Opening the door, he could see the fresh blanket of snow on the ground.

As he turned the corner, he found himself face to face with a bear. Jeff gulped. He froze, pondering what he should do at this moment. The bear looked at the ground and began pawing around. Jeff knew this was his only moment, so he jumped and ran to the front door.

He slammed the door shut. Nothing happened. Jeff crept to the window and peered outside. The bear was still standing there as if nothing had happened.

"What are you doing, Jeff?" asked his mother sleepily.

"Oh, playing hide-and-seek," explained Jeff.

"At this hour?" grumbled his dad. "Why don't you get some firewood?"

"Oh, I tried," said Jeff. He jumped on his parents' bed and said, "We are going to have to get warm the old-fashioned way. I don't think the bear outside wants to share the firewood."

"Huh?" asked Jeff's mother. Jeff just dove deeper in the blankets. He knew there was no way to get them to believe this!

STORY QUESTIONS

1. According to the story, you could determine that Jeff is . . .
   a. intelligent.
   b. immature.
   c. friendly.
   d. helpful.

2. Which paragraph helps you answer the previous question?
   a. second paragraph
   b. first paragraph
   c. fourth paragraph
   d. third paragraph

3. Why wouldn't Jeff's parents believe him about the bear?
   a. Bears aren't found in that part of the forest.
   b. Jeff told false stories a lot and couldn't be trusted.
   c. The bear never really existed.
   d. It is a rare thing to stand face to face with a bear.

Name _____   Date _____

NEIGHBORLY GHOSTS

Mary Beth had gone to spend the summer with her aunt. Aunt Lyddie had bought a very old house that was haunted. Mary Beth was both excited and nervous at the possibility of sleeping in a haunted house.

The first night, Mary Beth saw a figure in the mirror. It was just a glimpse, but she was sure she saw it. Aunt Lyddie saw a ghost in the pantry. Night after night, the sightings continued.

One morning over breakfast, Mary Beth asked, "Aunt Lyddie, are you afraid of the ghosts?"

"Oh, maybe a little bit, but it's all very exciting to own a haunted house," she said.

Mary Beth thought about that and then asked, "Why are the ghosts here? What do they want?"

"That's a very good question," responded Aunt Lyddie. "I intend to ask the museum curator when he makes a visit later today."

A few hours later, the museum curator came to the door. He came to examine some old artifacts Aunt Lyddie had found in the basement.

Aunt Lyddie couldn't wait a minute longer. "Tell us about the ghosts that live in this house."

"This house?" asked the curator. "This house isn't haunted. It's actually the house next door that's haunted."

"Oh," replied Aunt Lyddie as the curator left. Mary Beth was looking out the window. "Oh, look, Aunt Lyddie, I think I see a ghost in the neighbor's garden." That raised Aunt Lyddie's spirits, and off they went to find more ghosts next door.

STORY QUESTIONS

1. What is the meaning of the word *spirits* as used in this passage?
   a. ghosts
   b. trances
   c. feelings
   d. extraterrestrial beings

2. Which of the following traits best describes Aunt Lyddie?
   a. punctual
   b. scared
   c. shy
   d. adventurous

3. What is another good title for this story passage?
   a. "The Vacant House"
   b. "Haunted Happenings"
   c. "Mary Beth Learns Her Lesson"
   d. "The Ghosts Next Door"

LOST OWNER

Taylor and Gwen were excited the afternoon they found a lost dog. The dog was white and fluffy with thick fur. The girls had been hanging signs up around their apartment building trying to find the owner, but they didn't really want to find the owner.

"Lost dog," called Taylor.

The next morning, the dog followed Taylor to school. Taylor had to call her mom to come and get it. Gwen took the dog with her on her paper route that afternoon, asking customers if they recognized the dog.

That evening, they couldn't find the dog. The girls searched everywhere in the apartment, but the dog was missing. Just then, they heard a knock at the door. Mother opened the door to find a man standing there. "What can I do for you?" she asked.

"I've lost my white dog. I've searched for days and can't find it," he explained.

Taylor and Gwen's heart sank. "We used to know where it was," explained Mother, "but it has since vanished."

The man went on. "Well, would you be interested in the dog? Our family is moving, and we have to get rid of it. I wish I could have found the dog a home before we left."

"Yes!" screamed the girls. "The dog has a home here!"

"That is, if you can find the dog," reminded Mother.

"That's great," said the man, and he headed outside. The girls began searching again for the dog. That is, they began searching for *their* dog.

STORY QUESTIONS

1. According to the story, Taylor and Gwen are . . .
   a. bored and frustrated.
   b. hesitant about finding the owner.
   c. friends with the dog.
   d. going shopping when they find the owner.

2. Which paragraph first explains Taylor and Gwen's relationship?
   a. seventh paragraph
   b. first paragraph
   c. fourth paragraph
   d. third paragraph

3. At the end of the passage, Taylor and Gwen felt . . .
   a. disappointed.   c. frustrated.
   b. excited.   d. exhausted.

Name _____   **Date** _____

DINNER BY FIRELIGHT

Brett had told his mom that he would cook dinner tonight, but he wished he had chosen a different night. He had tons of homework and a science experiment to do. But there was no getting out of it. He had made a commitment.

Brett decided on frozen dinners. While fixing dinner, Brett was also doing his science experiment. He measured vinegar into a beaker and then added baking soda. The resulting explosion sent fluffy white stuff all over the counter. Brett tried to mop up the mess with paper towels before his mom walked in.

Brett turned around just in time to miss a paper towel catching on fire. It didn't take long for the small fire to catch onto some of the trash on the counter.

Brett's mother walked in at that moment. "What," she screamed, "is that?!"

Confused, Brett turned around to see the fire on the counter. "Well, that's my science experiment . . . I mean, dinner!"

Brett and his mom hastily put out the fire, grabbing water and dishtowels to extinguish it.

"Whew!" called Mom as she rested her head on the table. "This has definitely been a long day."

Brett's heart was still pounding. He placed a wet dishtowel over his arm and picked up what was left of the frozen dinner.

"Your dinner is served," said Brett as he took a bow.

His mother laughed and laughed. Brett went to get the phone number for pizza delivery.

STORY QUESTIONS

1. Which words best describe how Brett was feeling at the beginning of the passage?
   a. nervous and afraid
   b. happy and content
   c. relieved and afraid
   d. stressed and overwhelmed

2. Which sentence explains the problem in the story?
   a. Brett's mother walked in at that moment.
   b. He had tons of homework and a science experiment to do, but he had committed to making dinner.
   c. His mother laughed and laughed.
   d. Brett tried to mop up the mess with paper towels before his mom walked in.

3. What did Brett do that seemed to relax his mother in the situation?
   a. He tried to scare her.
   b. He was trying to defend himself.
   c. He used his sense of humor.
   d. He was trying to explain what happened.

Name _____ **Date** _____

MY SHADOW

Cade went to his locker to get out his books. Standing beside his locker was a boy Cade didn't recognize. Cade shut his locker and headed for class. On the way, he glanced behind him and could see the boy following him.

"Hey! What's up?" asked Cade's friend, Brian. Brian slapped Cade on the back while Cade hurried to his seat. The boy found a seat in the back.

The next hour things went the same. The boy followed Cade to his locker and then sat in the back of Cade's class. Cade was scared. Was he being stalked? He kept his eyes on the boy during lunch in the cafeteria. The boy kept looking at Cade.

After lunch, Cade got dressed for P.E. The boy stayed close to Cade the entire time. By this time, Cade had had it. He dropped the ball and marched out of the gym. When he got to the principal's office, he asked to speak to the principal. Mr. Jones stepped out of his office and motioned for Cade to come in.

Cade didn't waste a second, "Mr. Jones, there is a kid who is stalking me. He's been following me all day long. It's starting to freak me out." Principal Jones started chuckling. Cade interrupted, "Mr. Jones, this isn't laughing matter!"

"Did you forget that you signed up to mentor a new student?" asked Mr. Jones calmly.

The realization of what had happened flooded through Cade. He jumped up and ran out the door.

STORY QUESTIONS

1. What is the problem in this story?
   a. Cade doesn't know the name of the boy.
   b. Cade doesn't know why the boy is following him.
   c. Cade doesn't know why the boy doesn't introduce himself.
   d. Cade doesn't know why he is feeling so scared of the boy.

2. After reading the passage, which of the following statements would be something Cade would say?
   a. "Leave me alone!"
   b. "The principal better explain what's going on."
   c. "I wonder why this kid is following me."
   d. "Get away from me!"

3. Why did Cade jump up and run out of the principal's office?
   a. He was happy to get the kid off his back.
   b. He realized the mistake he had made and wanted to fix it.
   c. He was going to yell at the boy for following him.
   d. He was afraid to get a tardy in his next class.

DAILY Warm-Up 7

Name _____ Date _____

THE DOG ATE IT

"Where is it?" hollered Allison as she tossed pillows to the floor. "I have lost my homework again," she groaned.

"Calm down, Allison, you are freaking me out again. When you yell like that, I think something serious has happened," said her sister Katie.

Allison raced down the stairs, trying to find her backpack. "The teacher is going to give me an 'F' this time for sure," she yelled.

"Did you check in Dad's truck?" asked Katie.

Dad was just pulling out of the driveway. Allison went racing down the driveway waving her arms. It was too late: Dad sped off.

"Well, I hope it wasn't in there," panted Allison. She decided to check the laundry room. Sometimes she left her backpack in there as she came through the garage. She opened the door just in time to see their dog Snoopy leave a mess on the floor.

"Oh, Snoopy! How could you?" asked Allison as she began to clean up the mess. By the time she finished, she knew she only had a few minutes before the bus came around the corner.

"Katie! Help!" Allison was starting to panic. Katie calmly looked in closets, under beds, in the laundry chute, and on the dresser. She couldn't find it anywhere. "Allison's going to have to learn from this one," thought Katie as she put on her shoes. As she walked to the bus stop, Katie could hear Allison's shrieks and howls throughout the neighborhood.

STORY QUESTIONS

1. What does the phrase *"freaking me out"* mean as used in this story?
   a. You are annoying me.
   b. You are acting smarter than me.
   c. You are making me sick.
   d. You are scaring me.

2. Which sentence below explains the problem in this story?
   a. Dad was just pulling out of the driveway.
   b. "When you yell like that, I think something serious has happened."
   c. "I have lost my homework again," she groaned.
   d. Sometimes she left her backpack in there as she came through the garage.

3. What would be another good title for this story passage?
   a. "Helping Allison"
   b. "Allison Goes Crazy"
   c. "What a Mess!"
   d. "Lost, Not Found"

DAILY Name _____ Date _____

Warm-Up 8

THE BIG BUCK

Kenny loved to go hunting with his dad. It was a tradition, as they went every year. They planned their strategy each year hoping to catch the big buck.

This year, Kenny was old enough to get his own deer tag. He had passed the gun-safety classes offered for his age group. He was ready for this year's hunt like never before.

Kenny's dad went through the trees just ahead of him. They had seen some evidence of deer just over the hill, and they knew they were closing in on the search. All was quiet in the forest. Just then, a rustle was heard through the thicket. Kenny dashed through as quickly as he could. He had his hand on his rifle, ready to release at any moment. His dad veered off to the right, but Kenny stayed on the trail. He thought he caught a glimpse of some antlers through the trees.

There was another noise off to the left, and Kenny scurried on. His heart was pounding in his ears. Before he took another step, Kenny looked up and gasped. Standing directly above him was the big buck.

The buck was pawing the ground with his hoof, as if challenging Kenny. Kenny saw the rack of antlers swaying with weight. This was the moment of a lifetime. Kenny clutched his rifle again. He could not take his eyes off the buck. The two stared at each other. Kenny couldn't decide whether to shoot the deer or let it go.

STORY QUESTIONS

1. Who is the main character in this story?
   a. Kenny
   b. Kenny's dad
   c. the big buck

2. Which sentence explains the problem in the story?
   a. The buck was pawing the ground with his hoof, as if challenging Kenny.
   b. Kenny couldn't decide whether to shoot the deer or let it go.
   c. He could not take his eyes off the buck.
   d. His heart was pounding in his ears.

3. Where is the setting of the story?
   a. in a cabin
   b. in the woods
   c. on a rock
   d. in the mountains

THE RACE

Evan raced down the mountain as quickly as he could. He was determined to beat Steve to the bottom of the hill. As Evan swerved in and out of the skiers, he clenched his teeth. There was no time for a wreck today. Besides, his back still hurt from last week's wreck. The wind was now starting to pick up.

A skier yelled at Evan because he cut him off. Evan wondered if it was worth the risk. He felt like his time was quicker than last time—but was it enough to beat Steve?

Evan crossed over to where the ski runs merged back together. He glanced over his shoulder to see if Steve was behind him. No such luck.

"Where is he?" wondered Evan.

There was one more jump in the run that Evan had to make before he was home free. As he approached the jump, he saw a group of people standing around with other people sitting on the ground. Evan didn't have time to get a good look. He had his eyes set on the finish line. There was still no sign of Steve. He wasn't at the finish line waiting. That was unusual.

After stopping at the finish to catch his breath, Evan finally allowed himself to believe he had won the race! Only then did he look up at the crowd to see his friend Steve walking down the hill on crutches.

STORY QUESTIONS

1. According to the story, Steve and Evan are . . .
   a. friends.
   b. interesting.
   c. related.
   d. children.

2. Which sentence from the story would help you answer the previous question?
   a. Evan raced down the mountain as quickly as he could.
   b. He was determined to beat Steve to the bottom of the hill.
   c. A skier yelled at Evan because he cut him off.
   d. Only then did he look up at the crowd to see his friend Steve walking down the hill on crutches.

3. Why didn't Evan think that Steve might be hurt?
   a. Evan didn't really care about Steve but about winning.
   b. That would be unusual for Steve because he was such a good skier.
   c. Steve had told Evan he would meet him at a certain place.
   d. none of the above

IT'S ALL DOWNHILL

For her birthday, Carol had gotten a brand new scooter. Today was the day she decided to try it. She grabbed her library books and put them in her backpack. Carol began peddling down the hill towards the library. This was going to be a great day!

But Carol didn't realize that the hill was longer than it seemed. As she continued down the hill, she began going faster and faster. She also began to realize how little she knew about using a scooter.

On her bike, this trip was easy. Carol would just put a little pressure on her brakes to slow down. There wasn't a brake on her scooter. She was afraid to put her foot down on the scooter for fear that she would hit the ground and fly through the air.

Swoosh! The wheels were clicking, and Carol was starting to panic. How was she going to stop? Click, click, click . . .

Carol noticed a big bump in the road. She tried to remember if she should hit the bump aggressively or timidly.

Bump! The bump sent her flying through the air. This was going to be a rough ending. Things were going from bad to worse. She could see a car coming from her right. With her luck, she would probably hit the intersection at the exact same moment. Panic raced through Carol's body.

"How can I slow the scooter down?" she thought. Thoughts were racing through her mind.

STORY QUESTIONS

1. How did Carol feel about her scooter at the beginning of the passage?
   a. embarrassed
   b. excited
   c. frustrated
   d. expectant

2. Which paragraph would help you answer the previous question?
   a. second paragraph
   b. first paragraph
   c. fourth paragraph
   d. none of the above

3. What is the meaning of the word *aggressively* as used in the passage?
   a. forcefully
   b. quietly
   c. loudly
   d. angrily

THE MONSTER

Jared read every book there was about Gila monsters. The black and orange lizards intrigued him. He had even visited desert museums to see live specimens.

Imagine Jared's surprise when he happened upon a live Gila monster by accident. Jared had been traveling with a group of scouts in southern Arizona. He had wandered off the path to get a closer look at a cactus, when he looked down to see the lizard lurking.

Jared froze. He didn't dare move his body an inch. He knew that a Gila monster would take a bite and not let go. If the Gila monster didn't notice him, then maybe he could sneak away.

However, the Gila monster was staring right at Jared. It was frozen in mid-step, as if challenging Jared to make the first move. A drop of sweat dropped from Jared's forehead.

"What am I going to do?" thought Jared. His muscles were getting tired of standing still.

Just then, Mr. Carpenter, Jared's scout leader, grabbed Jared's arm and yanked him as hard as he could. They ran as fast as they could without stopping. Jared knew that his leader had saved him. He smiled when he thought of it. He turned to see if the Gila monster was following. There was no sign of it. That was the first time Jared could remember that he had distanced himself from a Gila monster on purpose.

STORY QUESTIONS

1. Which statement shows the climax of the story?
   a. "What am I going to do?"
   b. He knew that a Gila monster would take a bite and not let go.
   c. He looked down to see the lizard lurking.
   d. There was no sign of it.

2. What does the word *lurking* mean?
   a. projecting
   b. opening up
   c. observing
   d. creeping around

3. What is the main idea of the third paragraph?
   a. Jared is trying to get a better look at the snake.
   b. Jared encounters the Gila monster.
   c. Jared realizes he is in danger.
   d. none of the above

Name _____ Date _____

Warm-Up 12

A STROKE

Whitney lunged forward, reaching out as far as she could. She gasped for air and pushed forward again. Every breath felt like a stab in the heart. She had been practicing for weeks for this race. Every mind-numbing lap in the pool had been in preparation for this moment.

Whitney wondered where Lexie was in the race. Lexie had been Whitney's competitor for as long as she could remember. Lexie was an excellent swimmer. She had broken most of the school records— and she had only been swimming for three years!

Just over her shoulder, Whitney caught a glimpse of a red swimming cap. It was Lexie alright, and Whitney realized that she was just a stroke ahead of her. Was that really possible? Whitney's hopes soared. She poured her strength into her next stroke.

"Where is the end of the pool?" wondered Whitney. She could feel the intensity of the water being pushed back and forth by the swimmers. She slapped her hand on the wall and jumped out the water gasping for air.

Whitney kept her eyes glued to the scoreboard, waiting for the times. Yes! She had done it! By a mere second she had done it—but it was enough. She climbed out of the pool and looked over at Lexie.

For the first time, Lexie had the kindest look on her face as she said, "Good job, Whitney!" All of a sudden, winning no longer mattered. "Great race," replied Whitney, and she held out her hand.

STORY QUESTIONS

1. Which words describe Whitney in the story?
   a. new, outgoing, confident
   b. timid, shy, new
   c. determined, hard-working, anxious
   d. stuck up, timid, excited

2. Which information below is <u>not</u> shared in the story?
   a. Lexie and Whitney are not really friends.
   b. Whitney has been practicing very hard for the race.
   c. Lexie is new to swimming but doing very well.
   d. Whitney has doubts that she will be able to win.

3. What is the problem in the story?
   a. Whitney is feeling sorry for herself.
   b. Whitney felt like Lexie might win the race.
   c. Whitney has to really push hard to win the swim race.
   d. Whitney is nervous about beating Lexie.

RIM TO RIM

"I can't go on. Just leave me here," panted Branson. His legs felt as though they were no longer part of his body. He sat on the ground and stretched out his body.

"We can't leave you here," said Wendy. "Besides, we could all use a break right now."

The group of youngsters all found a spot to rest on the side of the mountain. The group had begun planning their journey many months before. Branson, Wendy, Chris, and Megan had all discussed the exciting possibility of hiking from rim to rim of the Grand Canyon. They had convinced Megan's dad to accompany them as their adult chaperone. Mr. Carter had hiked this very hike previously, and they were hoping to tap into his experience.

The group had taken many practice hikes to prepare themselves both physically and mentally. On the morning of the trip, Branson had awakened feeling sick. It was hard to tell whether it was fear or the flu. His body was not up to its typical strength, and he was suffering.

Wendy sat down by Branson and said, "Didn't we want to do this hike because we knew it would be hard? If it was easy, everyone would do it."

"Yeah," said Chris. "Besides, aren't we getting close to the halfway mark?"

"Okay, okay," said Branson. "I'm ready to go again."

The group rose to their feet, and Mr. Carter led the way. "Drink lots of water," he called out. Branson smiled and took a sip.

STORY QUESTIONS

1. What is the problem in the story?
   a. The group is not getting along very well.
   b. The group is trying to decide whether or not to continue the hike.
   c. The group is deciding whether or not to trust Mr. Carter.
   d. Branson is realizing the difficulty of the trip and fighting the urge to quit.

2. What would make another good title for this story?
   a. "The Dangerous Situation"
   b. "Branson vs. the Group"
   c. "A Call for Help"
   d. "Perseverance Pays"

3. What does the word *tap* mean as used in the passage?
   a. draw on
   b. fresh water
   c. depressed
   d. dank

UNEXPECTED DELAY

It was not unusual for the Judd family to take a drive on Sunday afternoons. This was a way for them to get Kendra, the youngest of them all, to take a nap. Maren was the oldest, and it was her job to sit next to Kendra in the car and rub her back so that she would get tired and drift off. It was a hard endeavor, but a plan worth pursuing.

Today's drive was one of the more beautiful excursions. The leaves were changing colors, and the sight was beautiful at every turn. Maren breathed in the crisp air and made a face at Kendra. Kendra barely noticed. She was starting to doze off.

As they rounded the next curve, the car gave a lurch and stopped.

"What?" asked Dad. He tried to start the engine again, but had no such luck. He glanced down at the gas gauge and let out a moan.

"Oh, no," he whispered.

"What's wrong?" asked Maren.

"We are out of gas," answered her dad.

"What are we going to do?" asked Maren's mom.

"I'm going to have to walk to town and get help," responded Maren's dad.

"That has to be miles from here!" said Maren in a concerned voice.

"We have no choice," answered Dad.

"No problem, Dad. I think your plan worked," answered Maren.

"It doesn't look like any plan is working," hesitated Dad.

"Oh, yes, sir. Kendra's asleep!" said Maren, and she put her own head back on the seat.

STORY QUESTIONS

1. What is this passage mainly about?
   a. how a family got lost
   b. the process a driver takes to get gas
   c. the different types of families
   d. how a family handles a crisis

2. In the second paragraph, what does the word *excursion* mean?
   a. intake of air   c. trip
   b. documentation   d. measurement

3. What type of word could be used to describe Maren in this passage?
   a. lazy   c. silly
   b. responsible   d. annoyed

DAILY
Warm-Up 15

Name _____ Date _____

FIGHTING WORDS

"Are you going to fight him?" asked Jason. "He's telling everyone that you two are going to fight after school."

Matt didn't say anything. Ever since Craig had moved to their school, he had taunted and teased Matt. Matt didn't know what he had ever done to provoke Craig, but he wished he could change it.

Both boys were on the same Little League team, and they were on the same all-star team. They both competed for the position of pitcher, and the position was given to Matt. Matt wondered if that was just too much for Craig, because since then, Craig had tried to fight him.

At 11 years old, Matt had never encountered anyone who wanted to fight him. He occasionally got into a scuffle with his brothers, but that was to be expected. Fighting a total stranger? What did that mean?

Matt closed his locker and headed off to class. His stomach was churning with anxiety. From out of nowhere, Matt felt a punch to his stomach. He lurched and let out a gasp. He looked up in time to see Craig pushing him against the lockers.

"Craig," he whispered.

"Yeah, what?" asked Craig. "I heard you've been telling people that you play better baseball than me. Is that true?"

"No," groaned Matt, "But I have been telling people that I better start practicing pitching so I can stay as pitcher."

"Really?" asked Craig.

"Oh, yeah," said Matt. "With a punch like that, you're sure to take my spot."

STORY QUESTIONS

1. What is the meaning of *lurched* as used in the passage?
   a. fell
   b. aligned
   c. staggered
   d. upset

2. What can you learn about Matt from reading this passage?
   a. He lives in a city.   c. He is creative.
   b. He loves to play all sports.   d. He is unfriendly.

3. Which of the following statements is accurate?
   a. Craig punched Matt in the nose.
   b. Matt was able to pin Craig and get him to stop fighting.
   c. Craig was upset with Matt for calling him names.
   d. none of the above

Fiction: Mystery/Suspense/Adventure

Name _____ **Date** _____

THE FOOTHOLD

Kirk reached up with his foot in search of another good foothold. He was surprised. He never dreamed he would be able to climb this high.

"Look at me, guys. Can you believe it?" called Kirk.

"Easy does it," called Kirk's dad. He was belaying Kirk, holding tightly to the rope. Kirk loved rock climbing. It was hard for Kirk to stay on the ground.

"Try to get up to the next level on the rock," encouraged Dad.

"I'm having a hard time finding a hold for my left hand," said Kirk.

"Go up a little further," said Dad. "There's a great hold just above you."

Kirk slid his hand into position and put his weight on the hold to pull himself up. Just as he did, his right foot slipped and he fell off the rock. He was dangling in the air with one hand still on the rock.

"Hold on!" called his dad. "I've got you."

"Ahhhh!" hollered Kirk.

Kirk continued to spin away from the rock, and he wondered if he was going to smash his head on the rock. He was glad he had his helmet on, but he wished he could do something for his stomach. It was spinning in circles.

Kirk's dad cranked on the rope, and Kirk came to a sudden stop. "Now, grab hold of the rock again," called his dad.

"I can't. I can't find a hold, and my head is spinning," called Kirk.

STORY QUESTIONS

1. Kirk has to have a great amount of _____ in his father.
   a. similar interests
   b. sacrifice
   c. trust
   d. understanding

2. According to the passage, what advice did Kirk's dad give him?
   a. Hang on tight to the rope.
   b. Let go and let the rope lower him.
   c. He wants him to climb higher to a ledge.
   d. He wants him to grab hold of the rock again.

3. The best way to find the answer to the previous question is to . . .
   a. reread the entire passage.
   b. reread the first paragraph and determine the main idea.
   c. reread the last two paragraphs.
   d. skim the passage and look for clues.

THE WAND

Tina was angry! She had tried to cast a spell at the king's ball but had been denied. "Can you imagine?" she thought, "Me! Just imagine that the most adorable fairy in the countryside is not allowed to cast her spell."

Just the thought of it made Tina's blood boil. Was it truly her fault that her wand had been bent and wouldn't work? King Trenton had grown tired, so when it came time for Tina, she had been dismissed after just five minutes. King Trenton wouldn't wait another second.

"Oh, what am I going to do? The humiliation of it all!" thought Tina.

Tina began trying to straighten her wand, hoping that it would help. She thought smugly to herself that the spell she was planning to cast was "prosperity." No other fairy had remembered to use that one.

"I bet the King will wish for that in a few years," thought Tina.

She pulled harder on her wand, when all of a sudden it snapped in two. Tina sat staring at what she had done. Did this mean she would never cast a spell again? Did that mean that she wasn't a fairy anymore? Why was she always in a mess?

Tina went straight to the head fairy's house and pounded on the door. She glanced at her watch to see that it was very late in the evening. Was it too late to call on the head fairy now? Tina cringed when she thought of creating another mishap this evening.

STORY QUESTIONS

1. What is the meaning of the spell "*prosperity*" that Tina was trying to cast?
   a. secrecy
   b. success
   c. humor
   d. peace

2. According to the passage, how did Tina's wand get bent?
   a. Tina broke it when she was trying to straighten it.
   b. Someone had sat on Tina's wand.
   c. Tina's sister bent the wand while she was playing with it.
   d. You can't tell by reading the passage.

3. The best way to find the answer to the previous question is to . . .
   a. reread the entire passage.
   b. skim the entire passage and determine the main idea.
   c. reread the second paragraph and search for clues.
   d. use context clues to determine the meaning.

ALIEN INVASION

Bounce! Bounce! Bounce! Ethan slowly opened one of his eyes. Who was bouncing on his bed? Between the crack of his eyelids, Ethan saw a little green figure jumping on his bed. Ethan closed his eye. There is no way a green figure could be jumping on his bed. Ethan opened both of his eyes this time and saw a green figure smiling at him.

"Onal;xnc," said the green creature.

Oh, wow! This is going to be a tough one to believe, thought Ethan to himself. He smiled and closed his eyes again. He needed time to think about this. Just then, he heard footsteps coming down the hall. It sounded like his mom.

"Ethan? What are you doing? Settle down in there," called his mom as she passed.

"Mom, it's not me!" yelled Ethan.

"Right, Ethan," answered Mom.

"I knew it," said Ethan. "Mom, come here!"

"Just a minute!" called Mom.

There was a look of panic on the face of the green creature. It seemed to sense something bad was going to happen. It hopped off the bed and scurried over to the closet door.

A few moments later, Ethan's mom came through the door.

"Okay, Ethan, let's hear your story," said Mom.

"Alright, here's my story: I woke up and there was a little green creature, sort of like an alien, sitting right on my bed," explained Ethan.

"Right," said Mom.

"You think I'm crazy, but look inside the closet and you will see proof!" said Ethan. Ethan's mom walked over to the closet and opened the door.

STORY QUESTIONS

1. A theme to this story could be . . .
   a. "There he goes again."
   b. "Make a wish, and it will come true."
   c. "If there's a will, there's a way."
   d. "Seeing is believing."

2. According to the passage, how did Ethan's mother feel about Ethan's story?
   a. She believed him.
   b. She made plans to see if he was right.
   c. She grounded Ethan for telling tall tales.
   d. none of the above

3. The best way to find the answer to the previous question is to . . .
   a. try to remember.
   b. reread the first paragraph and determine the main idea.
   c. reread the entire passage.
   d. skim the passage searching for clues about the mother's reaction.

Name _____ Date _____

READY, SET, FLOAT

Gregory invited his friend Jethro over to play a board game he got for his birthday. He was excited to play the game. He had read the directions last night in bed and could hardly sleep because it sounded so exciting.

Gregory waited at the window until he saw Jethro walking down the sidewalk.

"Yes! He's here!" whispered Gregory, and he thrust his fist in the air.

Jethro came in and took off his coat. He dusted the snowflakes off his collar. It had just started to snow.

Gregory had the game board set up with all the pieces. He immediately began explaining the rules and directions. Jethro nodded his head in understanding, and it wasn't long before the two were ready to begin.

Gregory rolled the die first. He began counting the number of spaces and saw that he landed on the "atmosphere space" on the game board. As Gregory set his token down on the space, he felt a strange sensation. Suddenly, he noticed his hair standing up in the air.

"What's going on?" asked Gregory. Soon he felt his hands rising upwards along with his body and his feet. Before he knew it, he was touching the ceiling.

"Oh, wow, " said Jethro in a stunned voice. "What happened? What are you doing?"

"I don't know," said Gregory. "You try it. Roll a six and land on this space. See what happens to you."

"This is freaky!" exclaimed Jethro, rolling the die.

STORY QUESTIONS

1. Which words could describe Gregory at one point in the story?
   a. confused
   b. annoyed
   c. furious
   d. coy

2. Which of the following statements is <u>not</u> accurate?
   a. Jethro was interested in playing the game with Gregory.
   b. Gregory was trying to scare Jethro.
   c. When Gregory landed on the space, he began floating in the air.
   d. There isn't an ending to this story.

3. What is the problem in the story?
   a. Gregory is feeling sorry for himself.
   b. Jethro thinks his friend is a little crazy.
   c. Something strange is happening while the boys are playing the game.
   d. Gregory is nervous about what his parents will think.

DOUBLE TROUBLE

"Mr. Franson, would you please send Samantha Jacobs to the principal's office?" the intercom announced without warning.

Mr. Franson looked up at Samantha and motioned towards the door. Samantha had a confused and scared look on her face. Why would the principal need to see her?

"It's okay," Mr. Franson said calmingly. "I'm sure he just has a question for you or a paper that needs to be signed. Hurry back so you can share your report."

Samantha slowly walked down the corridor towards the principal's office. She had made it all the way to fifth grade without being summoned here. Her mind was racing, trying to think of a reason why she needed to go now.

"There you are," said Principal Stewart. "I was hoping you were in school today. Come on in to my office."

Samantha followed Mr. Stewart inside and sat down.

"It seems we have something unusual going on," he said. You see, we had a new student report to school today, and she said that her name was Samantha Jacobs. The address she listed as her home address matches yours exactly. Her phone number is the same, as well."

"Mr. Stewart, I don't know what's going on. I've never heard of this Samantha," said Samantha.

"The interesting part is that we looked up the name Samantha Jacobs in the school records, and there was a Samantha Jacobs that attended this same school a hundred years ago," continued Mr. Stewart. Samantha's jaw dropped to the floor.

STORY QUESTIONS

1. According to the story, Samantha was sent to the principal's office because . . .
   a. she was caught cheating.
   b. she was being given an award.
   c. she was being questioned about a new student.
   d. she was being asked about a ghost.

2. Which sentence from the story would help you answer the previous question?
   a. "Mr. Franson, would you please send Samantha Jacobs to the principal's office?"
   b. "You see, we had a new student report to school today, and she said that her name was Samantha Jacobs."
   c. "There you are," said Principal Stewart.
   d. Samantha's jaw dropped to the floor.

3. What is the climax in this reading passage?
   a. Samantha is afraid of going to the principal's office.
   b. Samantha knew that she was going to be in trouble.
   c. Samantha was accused of having a twin at school.
   d. none of the above

REALIGNMENT

Slam! The door slammed behind Eldon as he climbed out of the car. The howl of the wind was intense. He tightened the coat around his waist. He tried to see the names of the stores. It was hard to see through the debris.

Eldon stopped at the third store on the street. Though he couldn't see the store sign, he knew that the bookstore was just past the coffee shop. This wasn't an ordinary bookstore; in fact, it only sold books that were out of print and unusual.

Eldon slipped inside and brushed his hair back into place. He let out a gasp when he surveyed the surroundings. There wasn't a single item in the place. Every book, chair, and shelf had been removed.

"What?" asked Eldon.

Just then, a man came from the back room. "Can I help you?"

"I was looking for the bookstore! It used to be here." The man looked wearily at Eldon.

"A bookstore?" he asked.

"Yes, The Cobblestone Bookstore," said Eldon as he walked back to check the sign outside. There wasn't a sign there at all. The only thing left were the nails that once held it in place.

"What did you do with the bookstore?" demanded Eldon.

"Young man, I don't know what you are talking about. We just bought this store. It's been vacant for years. My brother and I are trying to open up a second-hand store."

Eldon turned to run out the door, but it was locked.

STORY QUESTIONS

1. What is the meaning of the word *debris* as used in the passage?
   a. rubbish
   b. padding
   c. organized plant life
   d. wind gusts

2. What do you think will most likely happen next in the story?
   a. Eldon will attack the man.
   b. Eldon will call the mayor.
   c. Eldon will demand his money back.
   d. Eldon will get scared.

3. What is the main problem in the story?
   a. Eldon is lost and can't find his way.
   b. Eldon is upset because the bookstore is closed.
   c. Eldon is confused about what happened to the bookstore.
   d. none of the above

MESSY ROOM

It didn't take long for Jennie's room to get messy. She was always in a hurry. Her soccer jersey seemed to have a permanent home on the floor, and the garbage can seemed to be taking on a life of its own. Jennie's mom had tried every tactic in the book to get Jennie to clean her room, but it was to no avail.

One lazy afternoon, Jennie was in her bedroom with the instructions that she was not to come out until it was clean. After Jennie had been inside her room for about two hours, her little sister Nellie went to check on her. She knocked on the door: no answer. Nellie called, "Jen?" There was still no answer. Not knowing what else to do, Nellie went downstairs.

That night when it came time for dinner, Jennie's father called her down for dinner.

"Her room must really be a mess this time," said Mother calmly.

Sitting around the dining room table, Jennie's family began to eat their spaghetti. The family could hear someone calling, "Help!" They all looked at one another.

"That sounds like Jennie," said Nellie. The family jumped to their feet and ran up the stairs. They flung open the door to see Jennie's room still a pile of mess.

"Jennie, where are you?" asked Father.

"I'm under here," called Jennie. "I'm stuck in my dollhouse and can't get out!"

Jennie's family all knelt down and peered through the windows of the dollhouse. There sat a miniature Jennie on the dollhouse floor.

STORY QUESTIONS

1. Did Jennie really shrink to fit in the dollhouse?
   a. Yes. Her mother sent her to her room in the dollhouse.
   b. Yes. Somehow she shrunk while cleaning her room.
   c. No. Nellie just told her parents that's where she was.
   d. No. Jennie was making up the creature.

2. What is the meaning of the word *tactic* as used in the story?
   a. story   c. method
   b. tack   d. lengthy

3. What event in this story indicates that it is a fantasy story?
   a. eating spaghetti   c. no answer when called
   b. cleaning the room   d. Jennie fitting inside a dollhouse

JUST HER WAY

Mrs. Stuart hadn't missed a day of school yet, and so her class was surprised to find a substitute sitting in her chair one Monday morning.

"We have a substitute," breathed Jan.

"Maybe we should change our names," suggested Zack.

"Please have a seat immediately so I can take roll," interrupted the substitute.

The children filed into the room. The substitute wrote her name, "Mrs. Jesterway," on the board. Zack couldn't help noticing that when you broke up the sub's last name into smaller parts, it sounded like the words, "just her way."

Zack also noticed that her accent kept changing. Sometimes she sounded like she was from the South, and other times she sounded like she was from the East Coast. Zack decided to keep a closer eye on their substitute.

The substitute seemed a bit weird. Out of the corner of his eye, Zack noticed that the substitute was cleaning out her ears. This lady is something else, thought Zack.

An hour later, Zack saw the substitute turn a dial in the back of her head. He was getting more suspicious. Zack turned to his buddy Jake.

"Hey, Jake, did you see the sub crank a dial in her head?" Jake raised his eyes and shook his head. Zack looked back up at the substitute and saw an antenna rising out of her head.

"Jake! Look at that!" Zack called. Just then the substitute turned and glared at Zack. She began walking up the aisle to his seat.

STORY QUESTIONS

1. Which words best describe Zack in the story?
   a. creative, outgoing, confident
   b. timid, shy, new
   c. observant, worried, confused
   d. stuck up, timid, excited

2. Which of the following statements was an actual event from the story?
   a. Mrs. Stuart left a note for the class.
   b. The substitute was mean to the students.
   c. The principal reprimanded the students in Mrs. Stuart's class.
   d. Zack kept stealing looks at his substitute.

3. What is the problem in the story?
   a. Mrs. Jesterway is not a very good substitute.
   b. The class is having a hard time trusting Mrs. Jesterway.
   c. Zack is suspicious about the substitute's odd behavior.
   d. Zack is worried about what his friends will think if he gets in trouble.

KITCHEN PATROL

Sierra's mother called for Sierra to come do the dishes. This was Sierra's least-favorite job, and she groaned at the thought of it.

"Why don't we just use paper plates?" asked Sierra. Ever since the dishwasher had broken, Sierra dreaded the daily task of doing dishes. She hated everything about it—the dirty sponge, the grimy food on the plates, and the smelly dish soap.

That night, as Sierra cleared the table, she took special care to put the teakettle gently in the suds. As Sierra grabbed a sponge to wipe it clean, she felt an odd sensation. Wiping the teakettle with her sponge, a cloud of smoke filled the room.

"What is going on?" thought Sierra. She wiped again and another puff of smoke flew into the air.

Sierra set the teakettle on the counter and decided to ignore the incident. But as she picked up a plate, the plate began dripping a brown, muddy substance.

"Mom?" hollered Sierra. "I think our dishes have a problem!"

"What do you mean?" asked her mother.

"The dishes are making their own mess," said Sierra as she put down a fork that spewed white, cloudy mush.

"Sierra, we don't have time for games. Get the dishes done so we can leave," instructed Mother.

Just then, Sierra opened the broom closet to find a fountain of mud spraying out into the room. Sierra slammed the closet door shut and ran out of the room.

STORY QUESTIONS

1. What is the main idea of the first paragraph?
   a. It explains why the dishes are dirty.
   b. It contains the climax of the story.
   c. It shares the resolution about why the dishes were so dirty.
   d. It provides background and describes the story setting.

2. What can you learn about Sierra from reading this passage?
   a. She likes to do dishes.
   b. She wishes that her mom would help her in the kitchen.
   c. She lives a fantasy life.
   d. She is confused about what is going on.

3. Which of the following would make a good title for this story?
   a. "The Three Dishes"   c. "The Dirty Dishes"
   b. "Sierra and the Teakettle" d. "Mystery Mess"

COMPUTER LANGUAGE

Fritz was working early one Saturday morning when he noticed his computer doing some really peculiar things. Each time he would give his computer a command, the word *NO* would appear on the screen. The first time it happened, Fritz thought it was pretty funny.

"So you don't want to do what you're told?" laughed Fritz. He tried a few other commands and still got the same response. When Fritz told the computer to print, the word *NO* appeared. When Fritz told the computer to open the email, the same letters appeared again.

"What is going on?" asked Fritz. He no longer thought it was funny. Fritz scratched his head and shut down his computer. He was relieved to see the computer start to shut down. But it was taking a long time. He was frustrated with how long it was taking. He wanted to get the science report over with so that he could move on to more interesting things.

Once the computer was finally dark and quiet, Fritz booted it up again. Everything was happening as it was supposed to, until Fritz tried to open his word processor program. Those two little letters appeared again. Fritz stared at the computer.

Suddenly, he had an idea. Fritz slowly typed the following into the keyboard: "Yes you will." The letters appeared on the screen just as Fritz had typed them. Suddenly, he turned his computer off again. This was too much to comprehend. He couldn't actually believe he was talking with his computer!

STORY QUESTIONS

1. Which of the following could be a title for this story?
   a. "The Case of the Missing Computer"
   b. "The Day My Computer Crashed"
   c. "Invasion of the Computer"
   d. "The Computer that Could Talk"

2. What is the meaning of the word *peculiar* as used in the story?
   a. unusual
   b. similar
   c. surprising
   d. admiring

3. What sentence in this story indicates that it is a fantasy story?
   a. "What is going on?" asked Fritz.
   b. Each time he would give his computer a command, the word *NO* would appear on the screen.
   c. Once the computer was dark and quiet, Fritz booted it up again.
   d. Fritz slowly typed the following into the keyboard, "Yes you will."

"I WISH" SYNDROME

Byron was spoiled and always got his way. He even began throwing fits when he didn't get what he wanted. His parents were concerned but at a loss for what to do. It all came to a head on Saturday when Bryon woke up in a grouchy mood.

"I wish I had waffles for breakfast instead of cereal," commanded Byron.

Poof! A stack of waffles appeared on his plate. Byron was surprised and squealed with delight.

Later in the morning, Byron said, "I wish Jason could play today instead of being at his soccer game."

Poof! Jason showed up in Byron's living room with his soccer uniform on. Everyone was amazed. Byron's parents were perplexed and wondered what to do. Why was Byron getting his way? How could he make a wish and have it granted immediately?

Byron was starting to catch on to the magic of the words "I wish." Anything he wished for came to be. He began wishing for chocolate cake, a new bike, roller blades, and even a new dog. Poof! Poof! Poof! Every wish was granted.

Byron's parents were panicked. Byron began eating and playing and indulging in every single wish he could think of. It reached a point where Byron was exhausted from all the activities and lay sick on the couch from all the food.

"Oh, I just wish everything would go away," said Byron. In an instant, the living room was cleared and back to normal. Byron's parents breathed a huge sigh of relief.

STORY QUESTIONS

1. Which sentence shows that this is a fantasy story?
   a. Byron was spoiled and always got his way.
   b. "I wish I had waffles for breakfast instead of cereal," commanded Byron.
   c. Byron's parents were panicked.
   d. Anything he wished for came to be.

2. What is the meaning of the word *perplexed* as used in the story?
   a. honestly
   b. mystified
   c. easily
   d. carefully

3. Which of the following statements did <u>not</u> happen in the story?
   a. Byron forced others to give things to him.
   b. Everything that Byron wished for was granted.
   c. Byron's parents were worried about the granted wishes.
   d. Byron wished for a pair of roller blades.

SHHH!

Allison had awakened that morning at 5:00 A.M. That was exactly two hours before she had to be up, but she couldn't sleep. She was wide awake. It was in the early hours of the morning that she first heard a whisper. Someone was whispering something in her ear. She tossed the pillow off her head and sat up. No one was there. Allison figured that she must be hearing things.

She heard the whisper again on the school bus. She quickly turned around to see who was there.

"Did you hear that?" Allison asked her friend Lisa.

"What? I didn't hear anything!" replied Lisa.

"I keep hearing whispers in my head," confided Allison.

Allison wondered again if she was just hearing things. The whispers came again after fifth period. Allison was at her locker, and there was a lot of commotion going on with the other students. She was surprised that she could hear the whisper. It seemed to be directly inside her head.

Allison patiently went to class and ignored the whisper. The whisper was never quite clear enough for it's message to be understood, but it was loud enough to be annoying. At lunch, Allison determined that she would go to the school nurse and have her ears checked.

The school nurse checked Allison's ears and only found some wax. Just then, the fire alarm began blaring. The whispering got louder and louder inside Allison's head. She clasped her hands over her ears and scurried out with the rest of the students.

STORY QUESTIONS

1. What is the problem in this story?
   a. Allison is going insane.
   b. Allison is having a hard time getting people to trust her.
   c. Allison can't stop the annoying whispers in her head.
   d. Allison is having trouble with her friends.

2. What attribute does Allison display in this story?
   a. patience
   b. courage
   c. selfishness
   d. forgiveness

3. Which of the following statements is not a fact?
   a. Allison tossed the pillow off her head and sat up.
   b. Allison was determined to get the whispers to stop.
   c. Allison sees a doctor for help with the whispers.
   d. Allison wonders if she is just hearing things.

BLEACHED

Jenna washed out her paintbrush and took off her painting smock. It had been a busy day. Keeping the world all white was a busy job. Jenna was startled when her friend Crystal bolted through the door.

"That's enough!" said Crystal. "Aren't you tired of the same color? White is so boring and blah."

"I happen to like the color white. It's clean and pure," explained Jenna. Jenna had the power to determine the colors of the world. She had been given this gift at birth.

Crystal retorted, "But not everyone agrees! Many people would love to have a little color in their lives."

"Crystal, people clutter their lives with color," said Jenna.

"Color can also brighten spirits. Do you think you could splash a little color one day for me?" questioned Crystal.

"Alright, you choose the day," responded Jenna.

"Great!" cheered Crystal. "Do it on Monday. That's my birthday."

Early Monday morning, Jenna woke up and put on her painting smock. She mixed some color into her white paint. It had been a long time since she had done something like that. Mixing the yellow made her think happy thoughts. Making the blue made her feel peaceful and calm. The red was a fun color to mix! The black was a great contrast. Jenna was so excited by the time she was done.

Using the paint, Jenna painted a rainbow directly over Crystal's house. The colors were striking and beautiful.

"Happy birthday," she whispered. "Have a fun and colorful day."

STORY QUESTIONS

1. Jenna and Crystal are . . .
   a. enemies.   c. friends.
   b. students.   d. co-workers.

2. According to the passage, what does Jenna have against the other colors?
   a. She is allergic to other colors.
   b. She does not have the tools to make anything but white.
   c. She thinks that other colors clutter the world.
   d. She hasn't had training on how to make the colors.

3. The best way to find the answer to the previous question is to . . .
   a. reread the entire passage.
   b. skim the passage and determine the main idea.
   c. reread the fifth paragraph and search for clues.
   d. none of the above

Name _____ Date _____

THE NIGHT OWL

The alarm sounded at 10:00 P.M. sharp. Alex yawned and rolled over in his bed. He couldn't imagine that it was already time to begin his night. After a few more minutes, Alex got up and put on his pajamas. It wasn't long before he went downstairs for dinner.

"Yum! Those hamburgers smell terrific," said Alex.

"Thanks, Alex. Can you set the table?" asked Mom.

After dinner, Alex, who didn't want to, lackadaisically loaded his backpack for school.

"Don't forget your flashlight tonight. The weatherman says it's supposed to be pretty dark all evening. It isn't a full moon, either, so be careful!" said Mom.

"I will, Mom," assured Alex.

Alex headed off for school. He was awfully tired. He needed to go to bed later in the morning next time.

When it came time for evening recess, Alex and his friends played hide-and-seek in the dark. Alex tripped over a rock and scraped his leg. He didn't notice the blood on his leg until he came back into the classroom.

For midnight snack, all of the students ate graham crackers and milk. Alex was still hungry. He couldn't wait to go home for breakfast. Then he could eat as much as he wanted. At school, he was given only a small portion of food.

On the way home from school, Alex saw an owl and a bat. He was hoping to have a slumber party that afternoon. He planned to ask his mom if they could all stay up early.

STORY QUESTIONS

1. Which of the following could be a title for this reading passage?
   a. "From Day to Night" c. "Catching Some Sleep"
   b. "The Alarm Clock" d. "Reverse the Story"

2. What is the meaning of the word *lackadaisically* as used in this passage?
   a. annoyingly
   b. not excitedly
   c. questioningly
   d. ignorantly

3. Which of the following statements is an opinion?
   a. Alex planned to ask his mom if they could all stay up early.
   b. Alex has an interesting lifestyle.
   c. After dinner, Alex loaded his backpack.
   d. He needed to go to bed later in the morning next time.

NO MANNERS

It had been a crazy day at school. Jordan walked in and slid his backpack off his shoulder. He collapsed in a chair and gulped down a glass of milk.

"Pass the cookies," said Jordan.

"*Please*," insisted Mom.

"PLEASE pass the cookies," repeated Jordan. "I wish I never had to worry about manners."

"Interesting," said Mom as she left the room.

The next morning at breakfast, Jordan sat down to a plate of bacon and eggs.

"Yum!" said Jordan, and he piled the pancakes on his plate.

Suddenly, Dad reached over and grabbed the pancakes right off of Jordan's plate. Jordan was stunned. He was wondering what had happened to the *please*. Jordan noticed a black cloud covering his dad's face.

"Something strange is going on!" muttered Jordan.

A few seconds later, Mom downed a glass of orange juice and burped loudly. Jordan was flabbergasted. That was so unlike his mom. A black cloud covered her face, as well.

Jordan knew for sure that something was wrong with all the adults in his world when he showed up at school the next day and his teacher shoved his way through line, cutting in front of a bunch of teachers. The other teachers looked disgusted, and Jordan watched as another black cloud floated up in front of his teacher.

"Poor Mr. Smith," thought Jordan. "If only he would remember to use his manners!"

Jordan stopped fresh in his tracks. "Wait a minute," he thought. "I sound just like an adult. What is going on?"

STORY QUESTIONS

1. Which word describes Jordan in the story?
   a. confused   c. timid
   b. lazy   d. obtuse

2. Which of the following statements is <u>not</u> accurate?
   a. Jordan's parents were trying to trick him into using his manners.
   b. At first, Jordan is tired of using manners.
   c. A black cloud covered a person's face when they forgot to use manners.
   d. Jordan's parents are going to have to attend obedience school.

3. What is the problem in the story?
   a. Jordan hasn't learned his manners yet.
   b. Jordan embarrasses his parents.
   c. Jordan is confused by the adults' sudden lack of manners.
   d. Jordan is upset and angry with his parents.

HOLD THE PIZZA

"Chicken again?" complained Tressa. "We always eat the same stuff over and over."

"What's that?" asked Mom, smiling.

"Fish, chicken, lasagna—you name it. It's always the same old stuff!"

"If you had it your way, what would you eat?" questioned Mom.

Tressa had to think about it. "I would definitely choose pizza," Tressa grinned.

"Pizza, ugh!" Mom replied, "Go brush your teeth and head off to bed, Pizza Girl."

That night, Tressa went to bed dreaming of pizza. In the morning, she was surprised to find pizza on her plate for breakfast. She also found pizza on the school menu. When dinnertime came, Tressa winced when she saw pepperoni pizza on the table. She was starting to wonder if she was seeing things.

Tressa looked at her mom questioningly, but her mom didn't seem to think anything different was going on.

For the next few days, Tressa ate nothing but pizza. She was so sick of pepperoni. She thought she'd die if she ate one more pizza crust. Breakfast, lunch, and dinner—it was always the same. What was she going to do?

Tressa woke up bright and early the next morning. She got out the toaster and the frying pan. She cracked some eggs and stirred up some orange juice.

"What's going on?" asked Mom as she yawned.

"Breakfast," called Tressa ecstatically, "and I really mean breakfast!"

Mom grinned and pulled up a chair.

STORY QUESTIONS

1. What does *ecstatically* mean as used in this story?
   a. joyously   c. quizzically
   b. vertically   d. lamely

2. Which sentence hints at the resolution in the story?
   a. She got out the toaster and the frying pan.
   b. For the next few days, Tressa ate nothing but pizza.
   c. She was starting to wonder if she was seeing things.
   d. Mom grinned and pulled up a chair.

3. What is another title for this story passage?
   a. "Tressa Learns a Lesson"
   b. "Cooking in the Kitchen"
   c. "Too Many Cooks Spoil the Broth"
   d. "Pepperoni Pizzazz"

ANSWER KEY

Answer Key

Nonfiction

Animals

Page 9 June Bugs
1. c
2. d
3. b
4. d

Page 10 The Armadillo
1. c
2. b
3. c
4. d

Page 11 Llamas
1. d
2. a
3. c
4. d

Page 12 Sharks
1. c
2. d
3. a
4. b

Page 13 The Elephant
1. b
2. a
3. c
4. a

Page 14 The Boa Constrictor
1. c
2. d
3. d
4. c

Page 15 Penguins
1. d
2. c
3. d
4. c

Page 16 Zebras
1. c
2. b
3. a

Page 17 The Antelope
1. a
2. b
3. c
4. c

Page 18 The Koala
1. b
2. c
3. c

Page 19 The River Otter
1. c
2. b
3. c
4. a

Page 20 The Cottontail Rabbit
1. a
2. d
3. b

Page 21 The Red Fox
1. d
2. c
3. b
4. c

Page 22 The Crab Spider
1. c
2. d
3. d
4. b

Page 23 Harvest Mice
1. c
2. d
3. d
4. c

Page 24 The Sea Anemone
1. c
2. b
3. d
4. d

Biography

Page 25 Anne Sullivan
1. d
2. b
3. d

Page 26 Albert Einstein
1. b
2. a
3. c
4. d

Page 27 Franklin D. Roosevelt
1. b
2. d
3. a

Page 28 Louisa May Alcott
1. b
2. c
3. b
4. b

Answer Key

Page 29 Louis Braille
1. b
2. c
3. c
4. a

Page 30 Sacagawea
1. b
2. c
3. a
4. c

Page 31 Frank Sinatra
1. c
2. b
3. a
4. c

Page 32 Elizabeth Cady Stanton
1. a
2. b
3. d

Page 33 Daniel Boone
1. d
2. b
3. b
4. c

Page 34 Amelia Earhart
1. b
2. c
3. d
4. c

Page 35 Jackie Robinson
1. d
2. c
3. d
4. b

Page 36 Langston Hughes
1. b
2. c
3. d

Page 37 Anne Frank
1. b
2. d
3. b
4. b

Page 38 Leonardo da Vinci
1. c
2. d
3. b
4. b

Page 39 Robert E. Lee
1. c
2. b
3. d
4. c

Page 40 Wolfgang Amadeus Mozart
1. b
2. b
3. c
4. d

American History

Page 41 Battle of Antietam
1. d
2. b
3. d
4. c

Page 42 Thanksgiving
1. d
2. b
3. d

Page 43 War of 1812
1. d
2. b
3. d
4. c

Page 44 A Time of Reform
1. c
2. b
3. a

Page 45 Changes for Women
1. b
2. b
3. c

Page 46 Moving to the City
1. b
2. d
3. c
4. c

Page 47 Battle for the Alamo
1. d
2. d
3. b

Page 48 The Quakers
1. a
2. c
3. b

Page 49 The Women of Independence
1. d
2. a
3. b
4. b

Answer Key

Page 50 The Iran Hostage Crisis
1. b
2. a
3. d
4. d

Page 51 The Slave Trade
1. c
2. d
3. a
4. a

Page 52 A President Resigns
1. b
2. a
3. d

Page 53 The Korean War
1. d
2. b
3. a

Page 54 The *Lusitania*
1. a
2. d
3. b

Page 55 The Rise of the Common Man
1. c
2. a
3. b
4. c

Page 56 The Panama Canal
1. d
2. d
3. c

Science

Page 57 Saturn
1. a
2. c
3. d
4. b

Page 58 Geology
1. b
2. d
3. c

Page 59 Static Electricity
1. b
2. a
3. d
4. b

Page 60 Volcanoes
1. b
2. c
3. d
4. b

Page 61 The Rain Forest
1. d
2. a
3. d

Page 62 The Polar Regions
1. b
2. b
3. a
4. c

Page 63 The Telescope
1. b
2. c
3. d

Page 64 Waves
1. a
2. d
3. c

Page 65 Fossils
1. b
2. b
3. d
4. c

Page 66 Latitude and Longitude
1. b
2. c
3. a

Page 67 Desert Life
1. b
2. c
3. c
4. c

Page 68 Pluto
1. d
2. b
3. c
4. c

Page 69 On the Mountain Top
1. d
2. c
3. c

Page 70 Acids and Bases
1. d
2. b
3. a
4. b

Answer Key

Page 71 Cricket Temperature
1. c
2. a
3. d
4. d

Current Events

Page 72 PG-13 Movies
1. c
2. c
3. d

Page 73 Sixth Grade Education
1. d
2. b
3. a

Page 74 Skateboard Park
1. d
2. a
3. d

Page 75 Fix the Library
1. b
2. a
3. c

Page 76 Improving Recess
1. d
2. c
3. d

Page 77 School Conditions
1. c
2. b
3. a

Page 78 Teacher Salaries
1. c
2. b
3. b

Page 79 Lunch Choices
1. a
2. d
3. c

Page 80 Too Much Fundraising
1. d
2. a
3. d

Page 81 After-School Activities
1. b
2. c
3. c

Page 82 Take the Test
1. d
2. a
3. a

Page 83 School Assemblies
1. a
2. c
3. d

Page 84 Email Messaging
1. d
2. c
3. b

Page 85 Room for Art
1. d
2. b
3. a

Page 86 Female Sports
1. a
2. d
3. a

Fiction
Fairy Tales/Folklore

Page 89 Lesson Learned
1. c
2. c
3. a

Page 90 Crime Doesn't Pay
1. b
2. Instead of getting something for nothing, the fox ended up paying for his experience. He had to buy the costume, he had to pay for a parking ticket, and he was probably going to get a ticket for his reckless driving. He spent money and received nothing.
3. c

Page 91 The Loud Rabbits
1. a
2. c
3. b

Page 92 House Guests
1. c
2. c
3. a
4. a

Page 93 Lazy Bones
1. a
2. c
3. a

Answer Key

Page 94   Stick Together

1. c
2. b
3. As long as the bulls worked together, they were able to outsmart the lion. As soon as they started fighting and separated, they were not able to fight off the lion. Alone they were helpless; together they were strong.

Page 95   Well Said

1. b
2. a
3. d

Page 96   Peer Pressure

1. c
2. d
3. d

Page 97   The Long Jump

1. c
2. c
3. d

Page 98   Pretty Song

1. c
2. a
3. c
4. b

Page 99   The Jealous Wolf

1. c
2. b
3. a

Page 100   The Old Man's Daughters

1. d
2. d
3. c

Page 101   Climbing High

1. d
2. a
3. b

Page 102   Good Fortune

1. b
2. d
3. a

Page 103   Plan B

1. b
2. d
3. c

Page 104   True Love

1. c
2. b
3. The old woman realized that she missed the old man. She didn't realize it when he was gone for a short while; she just noticed the work she had to do. When he was gone for a month, she realized that she wanted the old man back.

Historical Fiction

Page 105   Fire on the Prairie

1. d
2. a
3. c
4. a

Page 106   Firm in the Faith

1. c
2. b
3. b

Page 107   Face to Face

1. b
2. d
3. b

Page 108   A Good Book

1. Nellie's father did not believe that slaves should be educated or learn to read.
2. b
3. c

Page 109   A Safe Landing

1. a
2. c
3. b

Page 110   The Christmas Gift

1. a
2. b
3. b

Page 111   The Substitute

1. a
2. b
3. c

Page 112   Herding Cattle

1. d
2. c
3. a

Page 113   Myreel's Moment

1. d
2. c
3. b

Page 114   Opening Up

1. a
2. a
3. d

Page 115   The Bull Ride

1. d
2. b
3. c

Page 116 First Aid Friendship
1. b
2. c
3. d

Page 117 I Am Japanese
1. a
2. b
3. c

Page 118 Blissful Gratitude
1. d
2. c
3. b

Page 119 Curious Joe
1. a
2. a
3. d

Contemporary Realistic Fiction

Page 120 Sky High
1. c
2. d
3. b

Page 121 Not Invited
1. a
2. b
3. d

Page 122 Snow Bunny
1. c
2. d
3. b

Page 123 Achoo!
1. a
2. b
3. b

Page 124 Math Whiz
1. d
2. a
3. b

Page 125 Daily News
1. c
2. d
3. d

Page 126 You Live in a Zoo
1. a
2. d
3. a

Page 127 The Dive
1. b
2. b
3. d

Page 128 Girls Just Want to Have Fun
1. b
2. c
3. a

Page 129 Stiff Stranger
1. d
2. d
3. c

Page 130 A Little Motivation
1. d
2. c
3. a

Page 131 The Goldfish Gulp
1. c
2. d
3. b

Page 132 Seth's Courage
1. c
2. b
3. c

Page 133 Dance Fever
1. d
2. c
3. a

Page 134 Teaspoon or Cup?
1. c
2. c
3. d

Page 135 Made in Mexico
1. b
2. c
3. c

Mystery/Suspense/Adventure

Page 136 Washed Ashore
1. b
2. a
3. d

Page 137 The Encounter
1. d
2. a
3. d

Page 138 Neighborly Ghosts
1. c
2. d
3. d

Page 139 Lost Owner
1. b
2. b
3. b

Page 140 Dinner by Firelight
1. d
2. b
3. c

Page 141 My Shadow
1. b
2. c
3. b

Page 142 The Dog Ate It
1. d
2. c
3. d

Page 143 The Big Buck
1. a
2. b
3. b

Page 144 The Race
1. a
2. d
3. b

Page 145 It's All Downhill
1. b
2. b
3. a

Page 146 The Monster
1. c
2. d
3. c

Page 147 A Stroke
1. c
2. a
3. c

Page 148 Rim to Rim
1. d
2. d
3. a

Page 149 Unexpected Delay
1. d
2. c
3. b

Page 150 Fighting Words
1. c
2. c
3. d

Page 151 The Foothold
1. c
2. d
3. c

Fantasy

Page 152 The Wand
1. b
2. d
3. c

Page 153 Alien Invasion
1. d
2. d
3. d

Page 154 Ready, Set, Float
1. a
2. b
3. c

Page 155 Double Trouble
1. c
2. b
3. d

Page 156 Realignment
1. a
2. d
3. c

Page 157 Messy Room
1. b
2. c
3. d

Page 158 Just Her Way
1. c
2. d
3. c

Page 159 Kitchen Patrol
1. d
2. d
3. c

Page 160 Computer Language
1. d
2. a
3. b

Page 161 "I Wish" Syndrome
1. d
2. b
3. a

Page 162 Shhh!
1. c
2. a
3. c

Page 163 Bleached
1. c
2. c
3. c

Page 164 The Night Owl
1. a
2. b
3. b

Page 165 No Manners
1. a
2. d
3. c

Page 166 Hold the Pizza
1. a
2. a
3. a

Leveling Chart

NONFICTION ▲ = below grade level ● = at grade level ■ = above grade level

Animals		Biography		American History		Science		Current Events	
Page 9	●	Page 25	■	Page 41	■	Page 57	●	Page 72	■
Page 10	●	Page 26	■	Page 42	■	Page 58	●	Page 73	■
Page 11	▲	Page 27	■	Page 43	●	Page 59	■	Page 74	■
Page 12	●	Page 28	■	Page 44	●	Page 60	■	Page 75	●
Page 13	●	Page 29	●	Page 45	■	Page 61	●	Page 76	■
Page 14	●	Page 30	■	Page 46	■	Page 62	●	Page 77	●
Page 15	●	Page 31	●	Page 47	■	Page 63	●	Page 78	■
Page 16	●	Page 32	■	Page 48	●	Page 64	▲	Page 79	●
Page 17	●	Page 33	●	Page 49	■	Page 65	●	Page 80	■
Page 18	●	Page 34	■	Page 50	■	Page 66	■	Page 81	■
Page 19	●	Page 35	■	Page 51	●	Page 67	■	Page 82	■
Page 20	■	Page 36	■	Page 52	■	Page 68	■	Page 83	■
Page 21	●	Page 37	■	Page 53	●	Page 69	●	Page 84	■
Page 22	●	Page 38	●	Page 54	■	Page 70	●	Page 85	■
Page 23	●	Page 39	●	Page 55	■	Page 71	●	Page 86	●
Page 24	●	Page 40	●	Page 56	■				

FICTION ▲ = below grade level ● = at grade level ■ = above grade level

Fairy Tales/ Folklore		Historical Fiction		Contemporary Realistic Fiction		Mystery/Suspense/ Adventure		Fantasy	
Page 89	▲	Page 105	▲	Page 120	▲	Page 136	▲	Page 152	▲
Page 90	▲	Page 106	▲	Page 121	▲	Page 137	▲	Page 153	▲
Page 91	▲	Page 107	▲	Page 122	▲	Page 138	▲	Page 154	▲
Page 92	▲	Page 108	▲	Page 123	▲	Page 139	▲	Page 155	●
Page 93	▲	Page 109	▲	Page 124	▲	Page 140	▲	Page 156	▲
Page 94	▲	Page 110	▲	Page 125	▲	Page 141	▲	Page 157	▲
Page 95	▲	Page 111	▲	Page 126	▲	Page 142	▲	Page 158	▲
Page 96	▲	Page 112	▲	Page 127	●	Page 143	▲	Page 159	●
Page 97	▲	Page 113	●	Page 128	▲	Page 144	▲	Page 160	●
Page 98	▲	Page 114	●	Page 129	▲	Page 145	▲	Page 161	▲
Page 99	▲	Page 115	▲	Page 130	▲	Page 146	●	Page 162	▲
Page 100	▲	Page 116	▲	Page 131	▲	Page 147	▲	Page 163	▲
Page 101	▲	Page 117	▲	Page 132	▲	Page 148	▲	Page 164	▲
Page 102	▲	Page 118	▲	Page 133	▲	Page 149	▲	Page 165	▲
Page 103	▲	Page 119	▲	Page 134	▲	Page 150	▲	Page 166	▲
Page 104	▲			Page 135	●	Page 151	▲		

Certificate

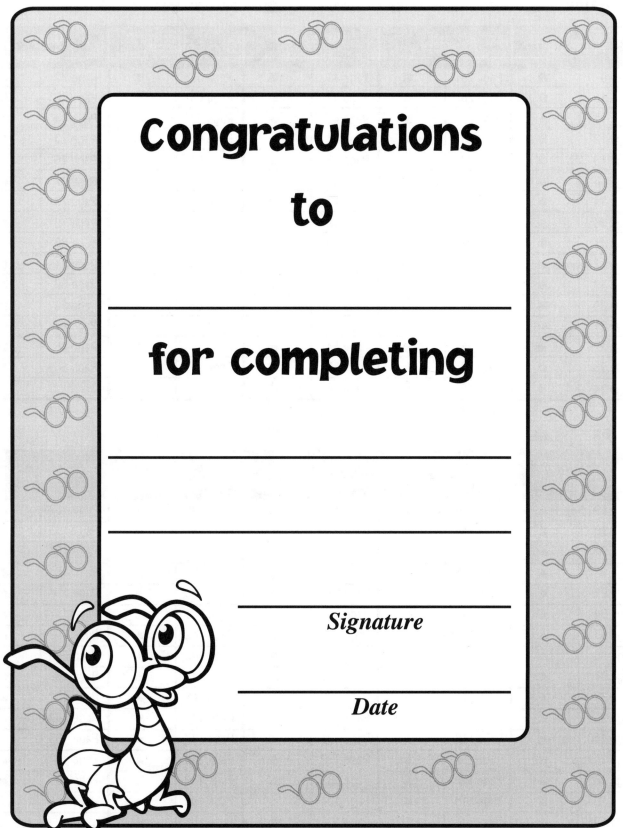

Congratulations
to

_____

for completing

_____

_____

_____
Signature

_____
Date